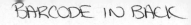

TRIBAL CHILDHOOD

Growing up in Traditional Native America

Adolf Hungrywolf

Native Voices
Summertown, Tennessee

ISBN 978-1-57067-213-2

Native Voices

Book Publishing Company
P.O. Box 99
Summertown, TN 38483
1-888-260-8458
www.bookpubco.com

Cover photo: Edward S. Curtis c1908
Woman and Child, Apsaroke tribe
Edward S. Curtis Collection, Library of Congress
Cover design: Sal Jefferson

Printed in Canada

Library of Congress Cataloging-in-Publication Data

Hungrywolf, Adolf, 1944-
    Tribal childhood: growing up in traditional Native America / Adolf Hungrywolf.
        p. cm.
    ISBN 978-1-57067-213-2
    1. Indian children--North America. 2. Indians of North America--Social life and customs. 3. Indians of North America--Folklore. 4. Birth customs--North America. 5. Child rearing--North America. 6. Family--North America. 7. North America--Social life and customs. 8. North America--Folklore. I. Title.
    E98.C5H86 2008
    970.004'97--dc22

                        2007052695

Native Voices is a member of Green Press Initiative. We chose to print this title on paper with postconsumer recycled content, processed without chlorine, which saved the following natural resources:

470 pounds of solid waste	3,010 gallons of water
9,951 pounds of greenhouse gases	7 trees
6 million BTU of energy	

For more information, visit <www.greenpressinitiative.org>. Savings calculations thanks to the Environmental Defense Paper Calculator, <www.papercalculator.org>.

TRIBAL

CHILDHOOD

CONTENTS

INTRODUCTION   6

A CHILD IS BORN 9

Winnebago Birthing, Naming, and Adoption * Flathead-Salish Childbirth * The Naming Feast * Flathead-Salish Naming Customs * Chippewa Life cycle * Parents and Children * Early Childhood among the Flathead-Salish * Life Cycle Among the Plains Cree

GROWING UP OUTDOORS 41

Training of a Flathead-Salish Girl * Omaha Care and Training of Children * Education among the Flathead-Salish * Ancestral Embers * Childhood among the Plains Cree * Gros Ventres Childhood

INITIATIONS TO TRIBAL MYSTERIES   81

A Winnebago Boy's Initiation * Poor Wolf Joins a Hidatsa Boy's Society * Daughters of Ponca Chiefs * A Girl Joins a Mandan Women's Society * Fasting Customs Among Winnebago Children * Omaha Ceremony to Honor a Young Girl * Children of the Iruska * A Sioux Boy as Heyoka *Clowns Among the Crow Tribe * Hosteen Klah: Boy Medicine Man of the Navajo

STAYING ALIVE   99

My Indian Grandmother * An Omaha Boy Gets Native Doctoring * A Hidatsa Childhood in the 1860s * Childhood Quotes

* Goodbird is Nearly Drowned * The Pawnee Girl Who Saved a
Prisoner * Riding a Dog Travois * Games Played by Omaha
Children * A Taos Schoolboy at Home for the Summer
* Chippewa Government of children

FINDING A MATE   135

Omaha Marriage Customs * Winnebago Marriage Customs
* Sioux Maiden's Feast * Hidatsa Courting Customs * Courting at
the Corn Harvest * Courting in Sioux Tipi Camps * Blackfoot
Tipi-Creeping on the Canadian Prairies * Plains Cree Customs
* Chippewa Puberty Customs

SOME CHILDHOOD STORIES   159

A Typical Summer Day for a Hidatsa Boy* Childhood Memories
of Willie Eagle Plume * The Debut of Aloyasius * The Return
* Little-Joe's Back Home * The Conversion of a Dozen Young
Hopis * Little Taos Boy at a Dance * A Sun Dance Child of the
Blackfeet

TALES FOR THE FIRESIDE   199

Manitoshaw, the Hunting Girl * The Poor Turkey Girl * Coyote
and the Fawn's Stars * Coyote and Crow * Blackfoot Legends:
Napi and the Great Spirit * Napi Makes Buffalo Laugh
* Napi and the Elk Skull * Origin of Names Among the
Cherokees * Why the Turkey is Bald * The Simple Happiness of a
Navajo Girl

EDITOR'S NOTE:

In this book the commentary of the author, Adolf Hungrywolf, is interspersed with historical text from archival documents, most written around the turn of the century. Some old terminology used in this archival material, such as "Indians," has not been edited, to preserve the integrity of the original writing.

To further distinguish the contemporary material from the historical texts, Adolf's comments have been set in the sans serif font shown here.

Historical material appears in the serif font shown here, and is introduced with a line identifying the source of the text. Sources are detailed in the bibliography at the end of the book.

Introduction

We are all Children of the Sun, and this book is meant as a tribute to all of us. From the Sun comes light and warmth to make life grow. All our human ancestors walked in awe of the Sun, although modern life often lets us—their descendants—forget about that.

North America's original Children of the Sun were native tribes who roamed the plains, mountains, forests, and desert sands, building simple homes and living in harmony with nature. Some of them did this so recently that being in awe of the Sun is still part of the heritage handed down among today's generations of native people.

By presenting in this book colorful narratives from earlier generations, it is not the intent to make you long for the past. We are now in the dawn of the twenty-first century; the world has been irrevocably changed from the childhood times recorded here. But the world's changes seem to have little value in helping our offspring feel like Children of the Sun, and that's too bad. So many children grow up feeling lost and alienated in today's world. These stories might help some of them—and their parents—better appreciate where we are all coming from.

These stories are especially for younger members of native tribes to encourage them to feel good about their native heritage, and also to remind them how closely they are descended from our land's original Children of the Sun. Young native people face the same daily challenges and distractions from modern life as their non-native neighbors and cousins. Public schools, television, popular music, complex toys, even the English language, have together captivated most native children so that there is little space left in their minds for thoughts about ancestral heritages and simple traditions.

People of all backgrounds can enjoy and learn from these stories. Everywhere there is a shortage of successful families to serve as role models for the young of today. Many of us parents want to make the lives of our children more meaningful than were our own, yet we have few examples to go by. Let these stories, then, be such examples.

The most important theme is that of families working closely together to survive the constant challenges of life. We still have constant challenges—though they may appear different at first glance from those of the tribal past—but we often face them as individuals, rather than as families united in the same cause.

Think of your family life as you read along. Are there things you could be doing with your family that might bring about a more united feeling? Camping is great for that; so is the planting, growing, and harvesting of food. How about building a home together, or part of one? All the families you're going to read about did these things together. They joined one another in frequent and sincere prayers, in wonderful sessions of singing and telling stories, and in journeys of adventure and discovery around their nearby lands. Families of today can still do all these things together, if they want to!

ONE   A Child is Born

A child is born. It is cleaned. The umbilical cord is coiled in a circle—a symbol of the circle of life—and tied. The midwife is careful not to cut this cord too short when she separates the child from its mother. Then she diapers the child, using an extra-soft piece of hand-tanned hide lined with a soft, absorbent plant, such as moss or sage, or else a layer of powdered buffalo dung. Then she wraps the child with a piece of old, soft hide, tying it with a leather cord. Finally, she gives it to the mother, who holds it to her breast for its first real taste of life.

That is the way our family's grandmothers described the birth of a Blackfoot child "back in the old days." Other native tribes had their own customs for childbirth, but there was a basic similarity to them all. They were simple, without much special comfort or glamour. There were no adjustable beds, drug injections, disposable diapers, or feeding formulas. It was childbirth at its most natural and sensuous, but also at its deadliest. In fact, infant mortality rates were so high in the old days that the stereotype of big native families crowded into tipis and lodges was certainly not due to husbands and wives having and raising many children! The average native woman appears to have thought herself lucky to raise three or four children to adulthood!

Once the child was born, mother and child experienced a unique sort of togetherness for a month, since tribal custom decreed that they should stay in seclusion until the passing of a moon, dressed in old clothes and avoiding social gatherings and public notice. This was a trying period for the health of the mother and child, back when life was often harsh and always rugged. It seems almost as though the tribe did not want to recognize the birthing until time showed it to have been successful.

At the end of its first moon, the child was given a "coming-out party." This could be quite an event, if things were going well for the family at that time, for they had to provide a feast and presents for guests. Relatives and elders were invited to the family lodge after it was first thoroughly cleaned by the family's women, and then purified with incense. Mother and child were dressed in new clothes for this special occasion. Everyone was given an opportunity to lavish praise and prayers upon the infant. Often the event was also used to announce its name, usually one given during that day by an especially notable person in the crowd. Gifts were given to the visitors, with the name-giver receiving the best and greatest number of them. In that way, the people came to know the new little persons within their midst, receiving a bit of happiness and reward at the same time.

The close interrelationship between young and old, as exemplified by the naming feast, is the key to success in traditional life. It is this key that is virtually unknown in so much of modern society, where youngsters often have little chance to know their own parents, much less a supporting cast of related elders. Count yourself very fortunate if your family life includes both children and elders.

Native elders say that young women have babies much more often now than they did back in the old days. There has been an unprecedented population growth among native tribes.

"Survival of the fittest" is no longer the basic theme of native life, at least not in the original sense. As parents (and as former children!), we can only be glad for that. But now, we must, instead, grapple with modern society's problems. Survival no longer means getting enough food and shelter, at least not for most native families; rather, it means a constant battle with myriads of distractions and problems unheard of back in the time of our great-grandparents.

A Wyandot Cradle Song

(Excerpt by Hen-toh from "The Red Man," Carlisle Indian School student newspaper, Carlisle, Pennsylvania, ca. 1925).

Hush thee and sleep, little one,
    The feathers on thy board sway to and fro;
The shadows reach far downward in the water,
    The great old owl is waking, day will go.

Sleep thee and dream, little one,
    The gentle branches swing you high and low;
The father far away among the hunters
    Has loosed his bow, is thinking of us now.

Rest thee and fear not, little one,
    Flitting fireflies come to light you on your way
To the fairy-land of dreams, while in the grasses
    The merry cricket chirps his happy lay.

Mother watches always o'er her little one,
    The great owl cannot harm you, slumber on
Till the pale light comes shooting from the eastward,
    And the twitter of the birds says night has gone.

Apache cradleboards

Chinook and dugout cradleboards

Winnebago Birthing, Naming, and Adoption

(Excerpt from Paul Radin, "The Winnebago Tribe," *Thirty-seventh Annual Report of the Bureau of American Ethnology*, Smithsonian Institution, Washington, DC, 1923).

When the time for delivery came, it was the custom for the woman to occupy a small lodge erected especially for her use. None of her male relatives were permitted to be present and her husband was not even permitted to stay at home. He was supposed to travel continually until the child was born, in the belief that by his movements he would help his wife in her delivery. According to one informant, the husband had to hunt game, the supposition being that this procedure on his part would cause his wife to have enough milk for the child. This traveling of the husband was called, therefore, "Looking for milk."

It was considered improper for a woman to cry out during labor pains. By doing so, she subjected herself to the jests of her elder female relatives. The positions commonly assumed by women in delivery may be described thus: Supported by the arms, which were passed over a pole held in the crotches of two forked sticks driven into the ground; suspended between two stakes; or flat on the back. The infant's navel string was cut off and sewed into a small bag, which was attached to the head of the cradleboard. The cradleboard was always made before the child was born.

On the birth of a child, the sisters of the husband were supposed to show his wife especial marks of courtesy. They always gave her valuable gifts, such as goods or a pony. They were glad that he had offspring, the people said, and even permitted their brother's wife to give the presents received from them to her own relatives. The presentation of these gifts was called, "Cradling-the-infant." Gifts were presented also to the wife's brothers.

Adoption of individuals was quite frequent among the Winnebago in former times. As far as the writer knows, however, it always took the form of replacing of a deceased child by some other child physically resembling the one lost.

A special feast could be given for adoption or it could be done at one of the regular feasts. As the child adopted was often the friend of the deceased, and in any case had parents living, presents were always given to his parents.

In the words of an informant: "When a child dies, then the father mourns for many years, and if during that time he happens to meet a child that resembles his dead child he asks to be allowed to adopt him. The parents of the child can hardly object to such a request."

LIFE IN NATURE: Tribal life meant being in the out-of-doors more or less all the time, since traditional homes were usually little more than shelters. That helped children to learn about the plants and animals that were always around. Wild pets were commonly kept—everything from ground squirrels and badgers, clear up to bears. A pair of bears lived for some years in the tipi of a famous Blackfoot chief.

This Woodland Cree household was photographed somewhere in the Canadian "bush" around 1925. It shows a content baby inside a typical Woodland cradleboard, the back made from two thin boards, the "rollbar" from a long, shaped strip of birch, and the bag itself, from striped linen or canvas. One lady holds a rabbit over the stitched birchbark home of a chicken, while the other lady has a store box turned into a cage for some poor captured owl. The family dog sits back in the shade, looking much on guard.

The Naming Feast

The clan name was generally bestowed on a child at a special feast held for the purpose. The bestowal of the clan name was not infrequently delayed by a father's inability to gather the requisite amount of food to be presented to the old man who was to select the name. Occasionally, it even happened that a father under such conditions permitted the relatives of his wife to bestow a name on a child, which of course was a name from its mother's clan. A person possessing no clan name was regarded as having low social standing.

Flathead-Salish Childbirth

(Harry Holbert Turney-High, "The Flathead Indians of Montana," *Memoirs of the American Anthropological Association*, Number 48, Menasha, Wisconsin, 1937)

Children wore the umbilical sack on a necklace after they learned to walk. This they did until they were grown. It was never thrown away or discarded. After a boy arrived at puberty and was ashamed of this ornament, his mother preserved the token for him. Girls, too, wore theirs until they were ashamed of it, such being a mark of childhood. They did not give theirs over to their mothers, but preserved it themselves. It seems to have been in the nature of a treasured memento in the case of adults, for in this late date it seems impossible to attach any calamity to its loss. It was always carefully guarded and was not discarded even after the death of its owner, but was kept among the family possessions as long as possible.

The birth being accomplished, the newborn baby was liberally powdered, its navel first having been salved with an ointment of beaver musk. The powder was made from the pulverized needles of a rather rare fir, and was applied to prevent the infant from getting sores.

Returning to the reclining mother: if all had gone well and the afterbirth had been promptly ejected as described below, the midwife collected her fee and went home. Female informants say that in the old days Salish mothers usually had trouble in ejecting the afterbirth. This they ascribe to the fact that the lodges were cold places in which to have babies, hence the blood of the afterbirth got thick and would not come out. The treatment for this consisted in gathering pine needles, heating them thoroughly at the fire, then piling them on the patient's belly. Fresh applications of hot needles were continued until the patient's interior was warm enough to thaw the blood so that the afterbirth would come out.

The afterbirth was the object of some fear. If the birth took place in summer it was merely wrapped in an old hide and taken out to be buried any place. But this casual procedure in winter would bring cold weather. Should it be buried in the lodge in a hole previously warmed with hot ashes before a final covering with earth, moderate weather could be expected for four days. Furthermore, the new parents must not wash during this four-day period lest the weather get colder. Care of the afterbirth was the last office of the midwife. Should the woman have difficulty, chills, or any other post-puerperal trouble, her family fed her a tea of *tsumtsumse* and *ntâg* to warm her blood and produce perspiration. A little *tsumtsumse* was drunk during the whole of the nursing period in order to medicate the child through the milk.

Some couples were notorious for their bad luck with children. Too many stillbirths or deaths in infancy would cause a couple to seek the help of a wise-woman. One interpreter, Mrs. Felicity Clark, who was fifty years old at this present writing, had seven children die in infancy. Her last two, Steve and Vincent Matt, grew up to healthy manhood because of the wise-woman's services. The medicine used was as follows.

When the old woman heard that Felicity was carrying her eighth child she came to visit her at her home in the Jocko. She said, "Your children need punishment. Let me take charge, and do not interfere if I treat them mean. No matter how it hurts your heart, let me treat them mean and they will live.'"

So upon the birth of the child it received none of the careful attention mentioned above. The midwife took it as soon as the cord was cut and cast it on a dirty, worn-out saddle blanket. Regardless of the objections of the mother, the baby was wrapped in this filthy blanket. It was not picked up or fondled. The wise-woman, however, knelt before it and prayed to that baby to live and grow up. This was done for a long time. It was wrapped in this neglected blanket to punish that baby. Even light ceremonial whippings were administered for the same purpose.

After the midwife had thought that it had been "treated mean" long enough, it was given its bath, but it always was laid on dirty outworn materials. During its babyhood the mother was forbidden to show it marks of affection, make the customary little gifts and treats. It was never given anything but wornout ragged clothing, and was made to go barefoot except during the bitterest weather when someone's old cast-off shoes were given it. As soon as it was apparent that the dangerous age for infant mortality was passed, the mother was allowed to lavish upon the child the affection which had hitherto been forbidden. While Felicity is an intelligent woman and a devout Catholic, yet she points to Steve and Vincent who are husky young men, and recalls the seven dead who did not receive this treatment.

If the mother died before the child was born, no attempt was made to save the infant. It was considered to have died the moment the mother did.

Two days were considered very ample time for a mother to lie about and feel sorry for herself. A girl who remained inactive for three days was considered to have gone the limit.

It was customary to lavish gifts upon the newborn. All the relatives and friends who could make contributions did so, but it was particularly incumbent on the grandparents to be generous. The types of gifts varied, but a young colt, about the same age as the baby, was considered the birth-gift *par excellence*.

The mother's morning began with the care of her baby. Just as soon as she had returned from the stream where she bathed before dawn, she took it from the cradleboard and laid it on a soft robe where it could thrash its limbs about and acquire the exercise forbidden by the cradleboard. After breakfast she bathed and powdered it and replaced it in the board. Then the mother or one of the little girls sang to it and played with it until it fell asleep. The board was then stacked against a lodge pole until the infant awoke and demanded care. Needless to say the girl children of the lodge were a great help in caring for their infant brothers and sisters.

FLATHEAD-SALISH NAMING CUSTOMS

Within about two weeks of the child's birth its parent invited a small group of respectable elderly people to a feast to name the newborn. The parents set out the food, then retired. After eating, the old people went over a list of possible appropriate names. Ordinarily those considered related to war-honors of distinguished persons, or were names of specific ancestors. It is observable that two possible naming systems are involved: the first indicates the Plains, while the second suggests the North Pacific Coast.

Having determined upon a name, the elders ask the parents their opinion regarding its acceptability. If it is acceptable the name is conferred, and the elders depart after prayers for the child's success in life and its power to emulate the deeds of the past bearers of the name. There is a strong hint of the matrilinear encountered elsewhere in Flathead mores. Most informants assert that the name, if ancestral, was ordinarily taken from the maternal family. This cannot be taken as absolute or invariable. Indeed, a few informants deny it entirely. But whatever the solution of the problem, the child generally took its name from the maternal side *de facto*. They seem to have preferred the ancestral method, too.

Names were not necessarily permanent. One might change his name later in life at will. Some war-honor might suggest a change, or perhaps one might receive a direct injunction to do so by a Guardian.

Chippewa Life Cycle

(Frances Densmore, *Chippewa Customs*, Smithsonian Institution, Bureau of American Ethnology, Bulletin 86, Washington, DC 1929)

In the old days the Chippewa did not have large families, several informants stating that the average was two or three children. A mother had her infant constantly with her and the daily relation between mother and child was closer than in the white race.

If a baby was born during the night it was customary to notify the people by firing guns. Immediately the men of the father's gens and those of one other gens went to the wigwam and attempted to gain possession of the child, the father and the men of his gens defending the child against the other party. The child's relatives threw water, and sometimes a mixture of flour and water, on the attacking party, and the men fought and wrestled. It is said that "everybody was wringing wet" when the struggle was finished.

The men who secured the baby took it to the leader of the gens who carried it four times around the fire while the people sang a song, with words meaning: "We have caught the little bird." The parents gave presents to the men to secure possession of the baby. It was said: "This was done to make the child brave from hearing so much noise as soon as it was born."

It was the desire of the Chippewa that their children should be straight and vigorous, and to that end the mother began a child's training in early infancy. Two means were employed for this training as well as for convenience in taking care of the child. These were (1) the cradleboard and (2) a custom which arose after the Chippewa obtained cotton cloth and which may be designated as "pinning up the baby." With these forms of restraint they alternated periods of freedom when the child was "let out for exercise." It was frequently bathed but clear water was seldom used, a warm decoction of some strengthening herb being preferred for this purpose.

The cradleboard, in which a baby spent most of its time for the first year of its life, consisted of a board about 24 inches long with a curved piece of wood at one end to confine the child's feet and a hoop at right angles above the other end. A light rod was fastened loosely to one side of the cradleboard and to this were attached the two binding bands, about 6 inches wide, which were pinned or tied over the child. In the old days the upper end of the board was cut in points and painted red or blue, and the entire structure was held together by thongs. Inside the curved wood at the foot of the cradleboard was birch bark of the same shape filled with soft moss. The hoop above the child's head served as a support for a blanket in winter or for a thin cloth in summer, thus protecting the child's head from the weather. On this hoop were hung small articles intended as charms or for the child's amusement. The leather strap fastened near the hoop enabled the mother to carry it on her back. If she were carrying only a cradle the strap was across her chest, but if she were carrying a pack, she put the pack strap across her chest and the strap of the cradleboard across her forehead. The binding bands were formerly of list cloth and decorated only on the portion above the cradleboard, but as beads and worsted braid became more common the decoration was extended over the entire length. The women took great pride in the decoration of these bands. Strips of hide were used in early days to hold the bands in place; these were followed by flat woven braid about an inch wide, made of yarn, one such braid being tied over each band.

In old times a baby wore little or no clothing, being surrounded by moss, which, with the birch-bark tray, was removed when necessary. Wood moss was occasionally used, but the moss in most common use was that found in the cranberry marshes. It was dried over the fire to destroy insects, then rubbed and pulled apart until it was soft and light. In cold weather a baby's feet were wrapped in rabbit skin with the hair inside, or the soft down of cattails was placed around them. Care was taken that the arms as well as the legs and back should be straight, and the arms of a very young infant were fastened straight against its sides practically the entire time. When it was able to move its arms freely they were released above the binding bands for a little while at a time. The cradleboard afforded warmth and protection, and it is said that children cried to be put back in the cradleboard after being out of it for a time. A mother often released a child and let it play until it was tired, then she put it in the cradleboard to sleep. When the mother was at work or was walking the cradleboard usually was hung from her head, but if the baby were asleep or if the family were traveling it might be placed horizontally in her shawl and swung across her waist at the back. A mother might put a child to sleep by holding the cradleboard in front of her and rocking it by moving her feet from side to side. The cradleboard rested on her toes as she sat on the ground. Sometimes the cradleboard was put in an upright position near the mother when she was at work and the baby was entertained by watching her. When the child was old enough the cradleboard was put near the family at meals and the child given bits of food, or it was given a duck bone to keep it quiet. In recent times a rind of bacon was used for this purpose.

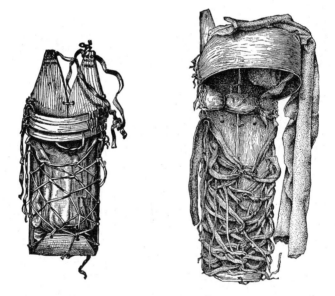

Navajo cradles collected in the late 1800s by Dr. R. W. Shufeldt. He describes the one on the left as "full-rigged of the poorer sort." The cradle on the right has a wooden hood and an awning of dressed buckskin.

If a child were "ailing" it was held in the warmth of the fire and its body rubbed with grease, goose oil being approved for this purpose. If it were too fat and chafed, a healing powder was made from rotten oak, rubbed to extreme fineness and freely applied. A baby was weaned by giving it fish broth or wild rice boiled very soft. Indian mothers, however, nursed their children until they were about 2 years old and instances are known in which a mother nursed two children at the same time, the older being 3 or 4 years old.

As soon as a child "knew anything" it was held up and "danced" while someone made a drumming sound like that of an Indian drum. This was done before a child could stand alone, and perhaps it is for this reason that very young children react immediately to the drumming of the fingers on a table or any similar sound. Chippewa women never allowed a baby to cry if this could be avoided by any mode of pacification and for this reason the small children were somewhat "spoiled." The devotion of a mother to her children was intense, and if necessary to defend them she fought with ferocity.

Three sorts of articles were hung on the hoop of a child's cradleboard : (1) Articles intended as "charms," (2) the article given to the child by the person who named it and which was supposed to convey a definite benefit, and (3) articles intended solely for the child's amusement. First among the "charms" should be noted the decorated case in which the umbilical cord of the child was preserved. Gagewin stated that the chief reason for this was the securing of wisdom for the child. Another said that if it were not done the child would become "foolish" and other informants said that if the cord were not kept the child "would always be searching for something." One said it would poke among the ashes around the fire, and older persons would say, "He is looking for the cord." It was desired that a child should play with this as it lay in its cradle and should keep it during its whole life, and for that reason the case in old times was sewed with sinew and hung from the hoop by nettle-stalk twines, both of which were very strong. This little case was treasured by a mother in the event of the death of a child. The writer knew a woman who had kept such a case for 25 years after the death of her infant son. A butterfly was sometimes embroidered or worked with beads on such a case, the butterfly being regarded as "the spirit of childish play." A similar case of plainer design was obtained from a woman who had kept it many years.

Two articles representing spider webs were usually hung on the hoop of a child's cradleboard, and it was said that "they catch everything evil as a spider's web catches and holds everything that comes in contact with it." These articles consist of wooden hoops about 3 _ inches in diameter filled with an imitation of a spider's web. In old times the web was made of nettle-stalk twine and colored dark red with the juice of bloodroot and the inner bark of tile wild plum. In a similar Pawnee charm the netting symbolized the Spider Woman, a deity who controlled the buffalo. In later times the web is made of dark-red yarn. Various playthings were given the child and suspended from the hoop, in easy reach of the little hands. Small white shells were favorite toys, also bunches of tiny cones made of birch bark. Sometimes one of these little cones filled with hard maple sugar was hung in such a manner that the child could put it to its mouth and get a little of the sweetness.

NAMING THE CHILD

The names of Chippewa under the old conditions of life may be divided into six general classes : (1) Dream name given ceremonially by a "namer", (2) dream name acquired by an individual, (3) "namesake name" given a child by its parents, (4) common name or nickname, (5) name of gens, and (6) euphonious name without any significance. In recent years there are also translations of Chippewa names into English, the adaptation of English names into Chippewa, and the mispronunciation, in English, of Chippewa names.

English names have been adopted into the Chippewa language and in some instances they have been so mispronounced that the original form is lost. Thus the French Josephette or Josephine has become Zozed, and Margaret has become Magid or Magidins, meaning literally "Little Margaret", Sophia becomes Sope, and Minnie becomes

Minin. In recent years the Chippewa have, in many instances, been known by the translation of their Native names, as Hole-in-the-day.

Soon after the birth of a child its parents selected a person to name the child. This person was called a namer and usually gave to the child a name connected with his or her dream. The bestowing of a name was not, however, the principal function of a namer. Indeed, the giving of a name was sometimes omitted. The principal function was the transmission to the child of the benefit which he or she derived from their dream. Odinigun, who had named several children, said that he always took the child in his arms and pressed it close to his body. He said that every namer did not do this, but he believed that more power was transmitted to the child by this action.

A child was given power by its namer, but it rested somewhat with the child whether this power was developed. Throughout the Indian's belief in spirit power we note the necessity of cooperation on the part of the individual in order that he might have the full benefit of that power. Odinigun related an incident of a woman whom he had known since they both were children. This woman's name was Me'dweë'ckwe (noise of wind in the trees). She was named in infancy by a man who told her parents that as soon as the child was able to walk the mother must take one of the child's dresses and hang it on a certain sort of tree. This must be done once a year. As soon as the child was old enough the mother instructed her to do this for herself. She continued this during her entire life and lived to be 95 years old. Odinigun said he had often seen the dress hanging on the tree, but knew nothing more than that the placing of it was a requirement of the woman's dream name.

The following account of the ceremonial naming of infants was given by Gagewin, a member of the Grand Medicine Society, who had named several children. He said that when the parents had decided on the namer they asked this person and a few others to a feast. The name of the child was not made known at this time, only that of the person who was to give the name. The namer put tobacco in the child's hand, saying that he (or she) would later give a feast and announce the name of the child. He asked all who were present to attend this feast and made a speech in which he expressed his appreciation of the honor conferred upon him. The time of this feast was indicated as several months in the future. Thus if the namer were chosen in the spring he usually gave the feast and named the child in the following autumn. As the season drew near he went to the parents of the child and told them the exact time of the feast at his house. He had already procured part of the necessary food and went at once to hunt for ducks and game. His wife got the wigwam ready, put fresh boughs on the ground, and had everything clean. She also provided dried berries, dried meat, and other adjuncts of the feast. Only five or six highly respected persons were invited.

When the people were assembled the namer told his dream and for the first time made known the name of the child. As already stated, this name expressed in some manner the substance or the story of his dream. Let us suppose the namer had seen a clear sky in his dream and that he intended to name the child Gage'anakwad, meaning "clear sky." He would have a right to say before the feast, "I invoke the spirit of the sky to make clear, fair skies for this child." If he had dreamed of an animal, he made a speech at the feast in which he dwelt at some length upon the power of that animal to guide and protect the child. If his dream were pertaining to some material object, as a bow and arrow, he told of the mysterious power that his dream had imparted to these articles. If he had dreamed of an event or of a mythical being, he explained its significance and told of the influence it would have on the life of the child. After the namer had talked and given a name, the other invited guests, as witnesses, signaled their approval and acceptance by "taking a few puffs" from a pipe. In this manner the namer conferred on a child what he believed to be its best equipment for a successful and upright life. Then followed the smoking of the pipe and the feast.

The gift of a small article representing the dream subject could be made at the feast but was usually postponed until a later day and the occasion for the presentation of the article might be an illness of the child. Its parents, anxious concerning its recovery, might summon the namer who would make an article suggesting his dream and bring it with him. He would first "talk over the child" then tell of his dreams, give medicine to the child, to bless it," and assure the parents that it would recover. Gagewin said that very sick children often recovered after this had been done.

Some parents neglected the naming of their children until illness overtook them. A namer was then summoned in haste, the belief being that his power could save the life of the child. Odinigun said that he had been summoned several times to name children that seemed near to death, and that the children in every instance recovered and lived to old age. He regretted that he had never been asked to name a child in health, as he felt that the power he could transmit to such a child would be of great benefit. His power and authority to name children were derived from one of his dreams.

Odinigun related the naming of a boy by a certain old man. When the child was about 10 years old he became so ill that the parents were afraid that he would die. So they sent tobacco to the old man and asked him to name the child. The old man came, looked at the child, and said he would name it the next day. He told the child's parents not to be afraid that the child would die before the next day. Most of the people assembled there did not believe that the child would live until night, but the man "talked and prayed" so the child would live until the next day. He gave tobacco to each of those present and told them to return the next day. He told the people that when he named the child they would hear a sharp sound of thunder. The child was alive when the old man came next day, and he named the child Ce'nawickun' ("He who produces a rattling sound with the movement of his being"). As soon as he had named the child they heard the sound as of sharp thunder, though there were no clouds in the sky and no sign of a storm. Many people talk of this event until this day. The child recovered and lived to old age.

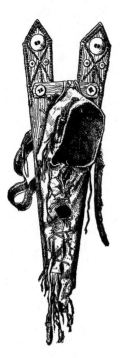

Blackfeet cradleboard

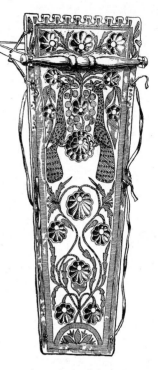

Iroquois cradleboard

Oglala cradleboard and mother

Parents and Children

The elders we've known all told us that it's good to have lots of children, so there will be someone around to look after you when you are old. Even in today's modernized native society, you seldom find old people left alone. In how many non-native towns would you find the still-common reservation scene of a young couple driving a flashy new car, while an old grandma sits in the backseat wearing headscarf and a shawl? Grandparents will even go to rock dances with their grandchildren. We know one who did so in his eighties, and he got out on the floor to dance!

In Blackfoot country, the name of a famous head chief of the buffalo days is still in use, because he adopted a little mixed-blood orphan boy who grew to old age and left a large family, which carries the chief's name as their own last name. Other children sometimes teased this boy because of his light skin and European features; they often called him "white man child." Whenever the boy went and told his father, there was always trouble for the teasers, since the man was head chief. He truly loved this light-skinned orphan boy.

This boy, incidentally, had a twin brother, who was adopted by a noted family among our northern Blackfoot division, the Siksika. Interestingly, both boys grew up to become tribal chiefs themselves, within their separate divisions.

There are many recorded instances of non-Indian children being adopted by Indian families. A famous example is the mother of Quannah Parker, himself a renowned chief of the Comanche at the end of the buffalo days. Cynthia Parker was a young girl when her parents were killed during an Indian raid. She was spared and brought to the Comanche camp, not as a slave, but to be raised with the other children of her captor, as part of his family. She later married a tribal leader, with whom she had Quannah Parker.

Although Indian tribal life emphasized love and need for children, there were also instances of child neglect, abuse, and even murder. In some of these cases tribal customs were involved, while others were the result of emergencies, such as enemy attacks or widespread starvation, as occurred now and then in the buffalo days.

For instance, a distant relative of our family's was a fearless warrior who sometimes brought his wife along on his enemy raids. We don't want to give his name because his descendants might not like this story, but it illustrates what kind of extremes the people were at times faced with—and perhaps still are today—among some hard-pressed people.

This relative was out on an open trail, traveling with his wife and a few others, searching for buffalo on the prairie. Before they knew it, they had wandered into the midst of a large and scattered enemy encampment. They were still unseen, so their only hope was to conceal themselves quickly in dense brush lining a nearby streambed and wait there until darkness would let them escape. For this, they knew they would have to remain completely silent and unseen.

Unfortunately, our relative's wife was quite pregnant at this time, and the excitement brought on labor. She gave birth right there, in hiding, to a lively and squalling child. Since people from the enemy camp were continually coming down near the hiding place for water, the group knew it was only a matter of time before someone would hear the baby's cries, and then they would all be discovered. Even if not then, the baby would likely attract attention from camp guards later on, when the group planned its escape. In addition, everyone needed to be ready for action at all times, which was not possible around a newborn baby. With much sorrow from the parents, the group together agreed that the newborn had to be smothered. Such circumstances were not unusual back in the wilderness days.

Children who were born with defects usually did not live long. If the mother saw that the deformity was hopeless, she often took the infant out to the bushes or forest and left it to die. Someone else might do this for her instead. Generally nothing was said against this in any tribes. The rugged lifestyle often left no choice in the matter.

Some particularly proud fathers wanted nothing but sons, and were known to order their wives to take girl infants outside and abandon them. There was a very old woman in the Blackfoot tribe, until just a few years ago, who was said to have been treated this way. Such action was tolerated, though not without criticism. Often the abandoned babies were taken up and adopted by relatives, or other adults, as was the case with the old lady of our acquaintance. Of course, there are also many legends about such babies being rescued and raised by wild animals, which might really have been possible back when everyone was completely wild.

It was not unusual for mothers, as well, to get sick or die from the effects of giving birth. The rugged lifestyle and lack of modern medical techniques left little room for difficulties. It was again a "survival of the fittest." If the infant stayed alive without its mother, it was usually given to another family with a new baby, at least long enough each day to nurse, though often permanently.

In this century there has been a population explosion among Indian tribes that has brought about drastic changes in lifestyles. Many factors have contributed to the increase, including better health and welfare and the elimination of many physical dangers. The strong influence of the Catholic Church among many tribes prevented the acceptance of birth control when it became available. Only in recent years has public education affected this trend, with the result that there are now new Indian generations who want to have only one or two children instead of a houseful.

Parenthood is planned these days, which is very different from the old way of having families, but there are still important events among many tribes for celebrating the birth of a new member. It is to be hoped that parents of today, who are able to choose when to have children and how many to have, will devote enough time and energy to making sure those children are well guided as they grow up.

Early Childhood among the Flathead-Salish

(Harry Holbert Turney-High, *The Flathead Indians of Montana*)

Very soon after birth children were treated with any number of charms. There seems to have been considerable variation in these nostrums among individual families. On the whole they seem to have followed the general Flathead pattern concerning charms noted elsewhere: the use of ointments prepared from the hearts of animals whose virtues were admired. Thus, an ointment prepared of lacerated mouse hearts mixed with clay, when rubbed on the male child's chest, would make him able to steal Blackfoot horses when grown. Again, a salve made of crushed ants and white clay would make the female child industrious in hunting and storing food.

Young children's features and limbs were constantly massaged and modeled to make them regular. The ears were pierced for future ornament at an early date. This was ordinarily performed by a skilled elderly person with a history of being able to do this without infection. The technique was simple. The elder prepared a small sharpened stick and slowly made the hole. An infection preventive existed in a tabu forbidding either the piercer or the pierced to eat another meal until the job was finished. In order to keep the resultant hole from healing over, a small greased twig was kept in the wound and slowly turned each day until it completely healed.

Babies' faces were also painted, but this was more to protect them from sunburn and cold than as a cosmetic practice.

Children were not weaned until they were three years old. Spoiled children might not be weaned even at that time. Modern children have been known to come home from school and demand the breast, only to be shamed out of the practice when this became known to their schoolmates.

There was never any idea that this prolongation of lactation prevented subsequent pregnancy. Indeed, Flathead women knew differently, for they did not cease to nurse the baby when they became pregnant again, or even after the new baby was born. They attempted to breast feed both or all their infants. They understood that this excessive breast feeding was a strain on the mother and that both children were undernourished, but nevertheless did not attempt to wean the other child.

Orphaned children were given to nurse to a woman who was carrying her own child at the breast. In a warrior tribe orphans were not uncommon. In fact babies of mothers who were going east with their hunting husbands were occasionally given to some stay-at-home relative to nurse, but everyone recognized that only a "good milking-woman" could perform this feat. It was not the standard procedure, however, to leave a nursing child in the west while the family went east on the Plains to hunt bison. It was rather the unusual which could be resorted to when occasion demanded.

The cradleboard used on the march was the traveling type, made considerably smaller than the standard variety. It is not thought that the stiff-backed, wood-reinforced cradleboard is very old among the Flathead.

The Kalispel maintain that long ago they did not use the cradleboard. They made skin bags of as fine a hide as they owned and lined it with the best and warmest fur. The baby was placed in this so that when the bag was laced he was completely covered except his face which protruded through a hole which was left for the purpose. This equipment was provided with loops of hide at the back so that the mother could slip them over her arms when she wished to carry the baby on trips. A tump line was also passed over the mother's head and under the bag to assist in this. All the Pend d'Oreille questioned on the matter say that the use of the cradleboard is quite recent among them, and that the Flathead are responsible for its introduction.

The back pad which was to protect the child from jolting whether the mother were afoot or ahorse was a bag of buckskin filled with bison fur sized somewhat larger than the hole in the base cover. The child bag was then sewn into an opening cut into the base cover. It was no more than a long strip of buckskin sewn so that it projected approximately at right angles to the base cover and was considerably larger than the baby. This strip was much fuller at the top so that when used it would form a sunshade over the baby's face. Flathead say that no board was ever lost from the saddle during a full gallop nor was a baby ever bounced out of its lacings.

Before the baby was placed in the carrier the bottom of the child bag was stuffed with pine moss. Then in the place where the child was to lie, from about its hips to this moss pad were placed many leaves of skunk cabbage. These skunk cabbage leaves are rather tubular in shape and were intended to convey the urine down to the pine moss where it was absorbed. Since the perambulatory child normally spent its day in the baby board, the leaves and the moss were frequently changed. Flathead claim that this lacing in the carrier is what gave them their fine erect carriage in former days and deprecate the careless posture of modern children.

Children among the Flathead are normally irritable, but when one becomes unusually bad-tempered, the mother suspects herself of a new pregnancy even though she has not yet felt any physiological indications.

Should this irritability pass without the mother's suspected pregnancy becoming assured, the occasion is passed over as unimportant. Yet the sympathy between the child in the cradleboard and the one in utero was considered very real. This bond was so great that the one already born was invariably a sickly, irritable, and squalling brat until the new one was delivered. The weeping one was crying for his brother to hurry and be born. When this happened "that baby got limber and is grouchy no more."

It hardly needs pointing out that being Indians, the Flathead treated children well. This does not mean that they allowed them to run wild, as reported among some tribes. A father's patience could be exhausted, and when he barked out a peremptory hoihoish, "Stop it!"

the nuisance generally ceased forthwith. It might also be pointed out that the Flathead had no scruple about spanking children. Yet it was considered very unwise to whip a small child as this produced an evil disposition. Character was considered formed around eight years, however, and the pre-adolescent pest's immunity ceased.

Misbehaving children were more often threatened with the supernatural than punished corporally. A favorite expression wherewith to frighten a child with an evil spirit was *"gage seme."* This term is impossible to translate, for "Cool supernatural" is not terrible in English. Particularly children were threatened with the dread village shamans. Owl and Coyote were also great child-frighteners.

There is also a clear tradition of a systematic frightening of naughty children by a personage called Spotted Face. Whether this individual was a specific camp bogey-man or just a member of the family is hard to tell.

He had one of his arms painted black and the other red, and he was armed with a red stick with which he would threaten to impale a refractory child. His face was made hideous by a mask of hide, horribly painted with livid spots.

The chief appointed a sort of child-policeman or group nurse, a guardian who kept them in order while their parents worked. This was an adult of any age known for his kindness and affection for children. He kept them out from under foot of workers, away from sacred objects or places, and in time of danger, close to camp. Except when the evening threatened, Flathead preferred to have the children shout and play away from camp.

Nevada Ute
cradleboards

Navajo mom and baby.

Life Cycle Among the Plains Cree

(David G. Mandelbaum, "The Plains Cree," *Anthropological Papers of the American Museum of Natural History*, Volume XXXVII, Part II, New York City, 1940)

Birth. No particular taboos were imposed during pregnancy. Several informants stated that a pregnant woman took care not to strain or over-exert herself, but that no prohibitions of a supernatural nature were observed. During childbirth, the woman kneeled against a chest-high support, made by lashing a pole across two forked uprights. Three women usually attended at birth. The head midwife stood behind the mother and massaged and supported her. Another received and cared for the newly born infant and cut the navel cord with a knife. The third was a younger woman who assisted the other two. The afterbirth was wrapped in an old piece of hide and hung on a tree in the forest. This was done to prevent it from being eaten by dogs. To induce an easy discharge of the placenta, a vessel of hot water was placed under the woman as she knelt.

The navel cord was cut at a point one hand grip and one thumb's breadth from the child's abdomen. The downy inside if the prairie puffball (*Lycoperdon Gemmatum Batsch*) was packed over the infant's navel and held in place by a bandage. The knife with which the cord was cut was not used again until the navel had healed over. The cord was later placed in an ornamented bag which the child wore around its neck.

The child was not bathed after delivery, but was dried with dry rotted wood or moss. Leather from the top of an old tipi cover, soft and well smoked, was used to wrap infants. Mother's milk was squeezed on the child's eyes. The baby was not nursed until two days after birth. Until that time, the infant was permitted to suck a piece of hard fat pointed at one end.

There were no especial twin beliefs. The twin born last was considered to be the elder.

Several days after birth the child was placed in a moss bag made by folding an oblong piece of hide or cloth lengthwise and sewing one end. It was stuffed with dried moss, with rotted and crumbled wood, or with pulverized buffalo chips mixed with cat-tail down. Two perforated strips of hide were sewn on each side of the long opening and laces were drawn through them. When a child urinated or defecated in the bag, the moss was shaken out and a fresh supply of absorbent stuffed between the child's legs. Children were, and often still are, kept in the moss bag until they are able to toddle about.

Cradleboards were also used but, within the memory of the oldest informants, were purchased from the Hudson Bay Company. The trade cradleboards were rectangular and had a forward projecting arc of wood at the head. A U-shaped wooden rim set upright on the face of the board some four inches from its margins served as a holder in which the child, wrapped in the moss bag, was placed and lashed.

Names. Not long after a child was born its parents prepared a feast. They invited a number of people and especially an old man known to hare powerful supernatural guardians. Female children were usually named by some old woman renowned for her supernatural prowess. When the company assembled, the father formally asked the old man or woman to name the child and at the same time presented the shaman with a filled pipe and some cloth to offer to the spirit helpers. The old man lit the pipe and then prayed aloud to manito and to the power who had inspired the name to be bestowed. After the shaman had spoken he sang one of his power songs. Then he asked for the child, took it in his arms, and pronounced its name. The name was derived from an incident or a character in one of the shaman's visions. He asked the spirit guardian from whom the name had come to protect the child.

Then the infant was passed from arm to arm around the tipi. As each person took the baby, he held it for a moment, addressed it by name, and added a wish for its future happiness. The child thus was passed around to all the guests until it reached its mother. Then the food was eaten and the ceremony so concluded.

A special relationship existed between a person and the man who had named him. The two called each other nikweme, and seem to have maintained something of the grandparent-grandchild relationship. In the ceremony accompanying the painting of a tipi cover, the man who had named the owner of the tipi led the procedure. If the child fell ill, its parents might call in a shaman other than the original namer to bestow another name. The former name was not abandoned and the child thenceforward was known by both names.

The motive for renaming was not because the first name was unlucky, but that the child might receive additional supernatural aid with another name and namer. Adults could not change their names in this way.

A grandfather could give one of his own names to his grandson in order that the boy might inherit some of its supernatural potency. The old man would let it be known that only the child was to be called by that particular name.

Nicknames based on personal attributes and foibles were freely given and commonly used. Fine-day recalled that, "Children would sometimes give each other nicknames in play and they would stick. I had a very good friend whose name was really Red-thunder. When we were small we used to call each other *nikowa't*. We would say, '*nikowa't*, let's go somewhere.' This is not a Cree word at all and means nothing. But it stuck to my friend and that is what he was always called. He was killed by the Pietas and the place where the battle occurred is known as 'The place where *nikowa't* was killed'."

Great fighters might name a child after one of their exploits in battle. Thus Chief Papwat named his infant son, Dragging-him, because he had once dragged a Blackfoot out of an entrenchment to the Cree lines in order to scalp him. But it was not usual to give such names and it was still rarer for a father to bestow a name on his own son.

A man who had performed a noteworthy deed or had had a remarkable experience in battle might be called by a name commemorative of the event. One such name was Strike-him-on-the-back, given to a warrior after a Gros Ventre had crept up behind him and brought a bow down on his back. A name of this kind was not formally bestowed, but was a matter of popular usage.

Sometimes a child was named for an unusual occurrence. Soon after Many-birds was born, her mother had propped the cradleboard against a tree and had gone off to attend to some task. When she returned, a great flock of birds had settled around the child and on her cradle. Because of this incident the child was known as Many-birds.

An eldest son often inherited his father's name, especially if the father had been a man of distinction. Again the name was not formally bestowed. The people of the camp simply called the son by his father's name.

It was considered impolite to ask a man for his name. Mrs. Paget ascribes the taboo against mentioning one's own name to the belief that the supernatural guardians from whom the name originated would be offended if the names were pronounced. However, a name that originated from a battle deed or from a peculiar incident could be freely uttered. It was disrespectful to refer to a dead person by name. An exception was made in the case of famous fighters whose names were recalled and pronounced long after their deaths as a means of perpetuating their glory.

Early Childhood. The period during which children were nursed varied. Some women weaned their babies when they were about a year old; others kept them at the breast much longer. A child of four or five on a present-day reserve was seen to reach under his mother's dress for the breast and put it to his mouth. The fact that intercourse was supposed to cease until the child was weaned was a factor in curtailing the nursing period.

When a child was weaned, it was given a tough piece of meat to suck and put to sleep with a woman who was not its mother. The woman slept with a paunch full of soup next to her body. When the child awoke, she fed it the warm soup with a mussel shell spoon. A broth made of the scrapings from a buffalo hide was the first non-milk food given to infant. Later, a soup made of blood and berries was fed to the child. Mothers also chewed meat and vegetable foods thoroughly and placed them in their babies' mouths.

Lullabies had distinctive melodies and were usually sung to nonsense syllables.

As soon as a child was able to run about, a navel cord bag was tied around its neck so that it hung down the back. The bag, finely decorated with beads and quills, was about four inches long. It had two compartments; in one the cord was stored, the other was filled with tobacco. An old man or woman might call the child and take a pipeful of tobacco from the bag. Before the old person smoked the pipe, he would offer it to his spirit helpers and ask them to grant good fortune to the child. In this way the parents assured a continual round of supplication for their child. Not all boys and girls wore these bags, for only the wealthy could afford to keep them filled with tobacco. When the child reached puberty, the bag was discarded. Boys abandoned it in the woods when on a hunting trip; girls laid it on the ground when they went out to collect firewood.

FLORAL BEADED HOME: This Nez Perce baby's cradleboard is about as fancy as they get, with the whole top fully-beaded in a stylistic floral design. The lower part, with its lacing, is covered by embroidered silk, over which hang strings of beads and several pink conch shells.

FOR WORKING MOMS: The mothers of many tribes throughout the world have long used this method of carrying their babies when it was time to go out and work, whether gathering firewood, tanning hides, or moving camp.

This Crow mother, photographed about 1915, is just holding her shawl together where it crosses in front, but if she needs to have her hands free she will knot the shawl, or hold it with a strong safety pin. Of course, now and then some little one would manage to slither out through the bottom, though the mom's braids were often held like reins in the child's hands.

TWO GROWING UP OUTDOORS

C hildhood in tribal camps and villages flowed in very natural rhythms, without much of the structuring that often gives today's children stress. Indian children's relationships with family, friends, and spiritual matters were usually taught with very strict discipline, but most of their day was spent freely, learning to flow with their big, outdoor world of nature.

Traditional camp life provided children with role models—heroes and heroines—who helped set and maintain high standards in many tribes. Brave warriors and hunters, wise chiefs, and sacred women were all held in high public esteem, so that most of the tribe's children strove to emulate them.

Of course, back then the requirements for success in life were quite basic and simple: Get food, have warm clothing and shelter, protect the tribe from enemies and bad weather. It didn't take a school degree to learn that, although tests were frequently given and failures often punished by death!

Those are still our basic needs in life, today, but modern children are often so distracted by all our material accumulations that they hardly recognize basic needs. Among some tribes there are predictions of a major event coming soon to the world to remind everyone of basic needs, again. How would today's youth fare in the event of a catastrophe?

Camp life was easily learned by every child, since it went on continually all around him. Children learned first by watching, then by imitating at play, and before too long by actual participation. Boys at ten or twelve were hunting, even fighting enemies, while girls of that age helped cook and tan hides, preparing soon to be married.

An infant's first introduction to discipline came in the form of cradleboards and moss bags. An Indian baby spent very little time unbuckled, lying out open, or left to crawl around in a big space. Scientists can probably make all sorts of deductions from the different practices, but we must at least recognize that children laced securely into bags start out life learning how to be still!

The cradleboard was a secure place for a baby to live during its transition from the mother's womb to walking about in the open world. For a people without cars and bassinettes, it was also a very compact and handy baby crib.

A moss bag resembles a soft shoe, made big enough for a baby to fit in and laced up the front with strings of buckskin. In the past these bags were made of hand-tanned deer and antelope skin, but in recent years some of the nicest ones were made of velvet.

A child's next discipline, after the moss bag and cradleboard, usually had to do with toilet training. This was started when a child was able to sit, and then encouraged even more when it began to crawl. Children able to walk were in all cases expected to make their toilet away from the home. Some parents told their children something like, "If you leave it close around here, the boogeyman will come after it and get you, too!" The enforcement of these practices varied from family to family and tribe to tribe, just as it does among all other people.

The act of first-walking was, itself, a cause for special celebration among some tribes. In one, this celebration was held when the child made its first lone journey on foot to a neighbor's home, that neighbor then being obligated to provide everyone with a feast.

Walking children were, of course, more troublesome than bundled-up infants, which is why some mothers kept their children in cradleboards pretty long. Other children around the household often provided supervision of toddlers, but certain rules had to be taught to small children very quickly if they were to survive. For instance, it usually required one, and only one burn, for a child to learn that it must stay back from fire. Other things were learned more slowly.

Physical punishment was not common in most Indian households. Because there were usually several grown-ups on hand, a disobedient child could expect quick disapproval, either in words or by sounds, such as *"tss-ss,"* which seemed to get attention about as quickly as a slap. In some tribes it was all right to slap a child, in others a willow stick was considered proper for the purpose, while among our own family's elders all forms of physical punishment were frowned upon for children.

A naughty Blackfoot child might hear a common threat like, "Hey, Coyote, come and eat this bad boy." Little children were quite familiar with the howling of elusive Mr. Coyote, and in their minds it seemed within reason that such a critter could be called in to bite them. Some tribes had a particular boogeyman, or another, whose name was called for help in settling a misbehaving child. Sometimes a neighbor dressed up and acted out the part, thereafter making the idea seem even more real.

One of our late family elders experienced a form of tribal discipline for children that no one practices today. Every morning, as a young boy, Willie Scraping White was forced to join a couple of others in a run to the nearest water, where they jumped in for a refreshing dip. This was especially vigorous when the wind was blowing, at twenty or thirty below, and a hole had been chopped through the ice to let them at the water!

Willie Scraping White lived to be ninety-seven, and he said this early practice toughened his body and helped him to grow so old. He said it also taught him to obey orders, since the morning ventures were supervised by an old man who walked with a long stick and was known for taking no nonsense. Besides teaching the boys to be brave and tough, this old man also taught them what might happen if they were to misbehave at some other time of the day. Scraping White considered himself and his friends always well behaved!

Religious discipline was of vital importance for the children of most tribes, since there were usually strict taboos against the mistreatment of religious ceremonies and articles. For instance, most Blackfoot households had one or more medicine bundles hanging at the back, in the place of honor. Children were taught from the start not to go near these, or to throw anything at them.

Yet, in the traditional home, children usually became involved in the family's spiritual practices right from the start, so that it was not long necessary to worry about their mistreatment. Instead, children acquired further self-discipline as they gladly sat and kept quiet for long periods at a time, in return for hearing stories and songs or for being allowed to watch their elders performing colorful ceremonies.

Religious teachings, like other training in Indian life, were passed on through the generations by means of active participation, beginning with earliest childhood. This is true of traditional lifestyles all over the world, including such more modern ones as farming and ranching, at least until recent times.

Child's hammock, Cape Breton

Young Hunter of Picuris

(An example of traditional Indian teaching is given in this excerpt from Ann Clark, *Young Hunter of Picuris*, Bureau of Indian Affairs booklet, Haskell Institute, Lawrence, Kansas, 1943)

They went outside.
In the clean snow,
Grandfather made
some turkey tracks.
Young Hunter was excited.
"I've seen those.
I know what they are," he shouted
and off he started running,
holding out in front of him
his bow and arrow.

Grandfather called after him,
"Are you picking berries
with the women
that you need to make such noise?
Perhaps you shout
to warn the game away
from such a dangerous hunter."

Young Hunter came back.
He stopped running and shouting.
He watched his grandfather.
He watched him taking quiet steps.
Then he, too, took quiet steps
and together they went
hunting for turkey.

Flathead Children

Training of a Flathead-Salish Girl

(Harry Holbert Turney-High, *The Flathead Indians of Montana*)

Our family used to have an adopted grandmother among the people of the Flathead tribe, who live south of us, in Montana. Mary Ann Combs was born in a tipi along Montana's Bitterroot River, in 1881. For the first ten years of her life she was among those few Flatheads, with her parents and other relatives, who shunned reservation life in favor of their ancestral wilderness homeland. In her old age, eighty or ninety years later, she was the last one of her tribe who had received the traditional training that brought her from childhood to becoming a woman.

Mary Ann grew up in the lodge of her grandparents, who wanted to make sure she would learn to be a woman in the true, proven, old Flathead way. Thus, when she reached puberty, they asked a highly respected old woman to be her guide. This woman, Mrs. Ninepipe, was noted for being a hard worker and a good wife and mother, as well as being kind and helpful to others in the tribe.

Mrs. Ninepipe went to visit Mary Ann early on the first morning of her instructions. She began with a lengthy prayer, asking that the girl have a long life as a good woman. Everyone who knew Mary Ann felt that this prayer came true. The woman gave Mary Ann additional blessings by painting her face with a red-colored earth that her people considered sacred.

Then she said, "You have to watch me and see how I live. I don't flirt or run around with men. I work hard to gather roots and berries, and to prepare all the meat that my husband brings home. I save everything I can and don't waste things. I know that my husband provides the family with food and protects us, so I follow his orders like a dog does its master, and I do what he wants me to do."

For the next four days Mary Ann stayed with Mrs. Ninepipe and did exactly as she was told to do. She was required to work hard during that time and she was not allowed to rest. Her father and mother warned that she should obey everything the old woman told her if she wanted to have the old woman's virtues in later life.

The people near her were part of a hunting camp of four lodges. She was required to bring a load of firewood to each of the lodges every day. She carried these loads on her back, in the old way. She was also told to bring the water supply for each lodge. In addition, she was required to do all the cooking in the lodge of her parents, without help from anyone else.

She said, "That old woman told me the reason she wants me to keep busy and working is so that I don't start out being a lazy woman, else I would have scabs all over my body—even on my face—and I would become lousy and filthy and would always want to lie around. I was pretty scared about being this way, so I kept busy all the time I was with that woman.

"'She taught me to prepare bitter roots the right way, and she told me never to be careless about it. She said to watch so that I don't waste food or let it get overcooked. She showed me how to make our traditional blood soup, without breaking up the blood too much. She said that if I was careless making this nutritious soup, the blood would turn into water.

"She told me not to warm my feet by the fire, else they would grow large as I got older. She said to warm a rock and hold it to my feet instead. You can see that I have small feet. She also told me that if I had any lice, I should take one and stick a pine needle through it and then stick the pine needle into the ground by the fire to roast the louse. She said that way I would never be bothered by lice, and she was right.

"Every morning I was told to get up very early and wash myself in the creek and put lots of water on my hair so that it would grow long and heavy [Mary Ann's thick, white braids still hung below her waist when she was in her eighties]. I was told not to wash with warm water or in a basin. That is why I still go down to the little creek behind my house every morning to wash."

Mary Ann was also given instructions for having children. She should never eat the flesh of the black bear or her breasts would go dry. Also, she was not to pick berries from bushes in which grizzly bears had fed, else the child she was carrying would always have saliva running from its mouth, like a bear.

She was told different ways of giving newborn babies certain characteristics, according to Flathead belief. To make a baby grow up quiet and gentle, she was to take the heart of a partridge, mix it with a certain white clay, and frequently rub the mixture on the child's chest. To make a child active, industrious, and grow up to be a good food hunter, she was told to crush a bunch of ants and mix them with white clay, to be rubbed on the child's chest. To make children brave, they should be rubbed with mixtures containing the hearts of hawks or eagles. To make them strong, the mixture should include part of a bear's heart. To make them good hikers and climbers, she should use the heart of an elk. Her husband, Louie Combs, had been rubbed with a mixture that included a chipmunk's heart, which made him always slim and frisky.

Mary Ann said that she continued helping old Mrs. Ninepipe for the rest of her life, in thanks for the guidance given her while she was young. In her own old age she believed that if the young people of today were still given such strict and direct training at the hands of elderly wise persons, they would grow up to have more respect for life and better behavior.

Omaha Care and Training of Children

(Excerpt from Alice C. Fletcher and Francis La Flesche, "The Omaha Tribe," vol. 2, Twenty-seventh Annual Report of the Bureau of Ethnology, Smithsonian Institution, Washington, DC, 1911)

In the Omaha family the children bore an important part; they were greatly desired and loved. The baby was its mother's constant companion, although other members of the family often helped to take care of it. More than one instance is recalled where the father took considerable care of the little ones and it was not an uncommon sight to see a father or grandfather soothe or amuse a fretful child.

Soon after birth the baby was laid in its own little bed. This was a board about 12 or 14 inches wide and 3 feet long. On this was laid a pillow stuffed with feathers, or the hair of the deer, over which were spread layers of soft skins. On this bed the baby was fastened by broad bands of soft skin, which in recent years were replaced by similar bands of calico or flannel. There was no headboard to the Omaha cradleboard, but the skins that were laid over the pillow were so arranged as to form a shelter and protection for the top of the baby's head. While the child slept, its arms were bound under the cover, but as soon as it awoke they were released.

The cradleboard was principally used in carrying the baby around and it served as a bed when the little one was asleep. A good portion of the time the baby lay on a soft skin in a safe warm place where it could kick and crow, while the mother sat by with her sewing or at some other employment. If the mother's duties took her out-of-doors, the baby might be laced on its cradle and hung up in the shade of a tree; or if the mother happened to be going away on horseback, the baby in its cradle was hung at her saddle, where it rode safely and comfortably.

When the child was old enough to cling to its mother it was thrown over her shoulder, where it hugged her tightly around the neck while she adjusted her robe or blanket. The robe worn by the woman was tied by a girdle around the waist, the upper part was placed over the clinging child, and the ends were crossed in front and tucked into the girdle. Then the mother gave a gentle but decided shrug, when the child loosened its arms and settled itself into its bag-like bed, from out of which it winked and peered at the world, or fell fast asleep as the mother trudged about her business.

It is a mistake to suppose that Indian babies never cry. They do cry, most lustily at times, but efforts are always made to soothe a child. Both men and women make a low murmuring that resembles some-what the sound of the wind in the pines, and sleep soon comes to the listener. There was a belief that certain persons were gifted with an understanding of' the various sounds made by a baby; so when a lit-tle one cried persistently, as if in distress, some one of these knowing people was sent for, to ascertain what troubled the child. Sometimes, it was said that the baby did not like its given name, and then the name would be changed.

The birth of twins was considered a sign that the mother was a kind woman. It was said, "Twins walk hand in hand around the world looking for a kind woman; when they find her, she becomes their mother."

As soon as a child could walk steadily, it passed through the cere-mony called "Turning the Child." If a boy, it passed through the sup-plemental ceremony of cutting the lock of hair in consecration of its life to the Thunder, and to the protection of the tribe as a warrior. After this experience, home training began in earnest.

Careful parents, particularly those who belonged to the better class, took great pains in the training of their children. They were taught to treat their elders with respect, to be particular in the use of the proper terms of relationship, to be peaceable with one another, and to obey their parents. Whipping was uncommon, and yet there was almost no quarreling and little downright disobedience. Much attention was given to inculcating grammatical use of the language and the proper pronunciation of words. There was no "baby talk." Politeness was instilled early-on. No child would think of interrupting an elder who was speaking, pestering anyone with questions, taking anything belonging to an older person without permission, or staring at anyone, particularly a stranger. Children were bright and had their share of curiosity, but they were trained not to be aggressive.

Little girls were subject to restraints that were not put upon the boys. The mother was particular in teaching the girl how to sit and how to rise from a sitting posture. A woman sat side-wise on the left, her legs drawn around closely to the right. No other posture was good form for a woman. Sometimes old women sat with the feet stretched out in front, but that was the privilege of age. All other attitudes, as kneeling and squatting, were only for temporary purposes. Concerning this point of etiquette, mothers were rigid in the training of their daughters. To rise well, one should spring up lightly, not with the help of both hands; one hand might be placed on the ground for the first movement.

A girl was taught to move about noiselessly as she passed in and out of the lodge. All her errands must be done silently. She must keep her hair neatly braided and her garments in order. At an early age, little girls assumed the role of caretaker of the younger children.

The boys had to help about the ponies, but not much training in etiquette fell to the lot of the boy—he could jump about and sit in any manner he chose—except after the fashion of a girl. Later he had to learn to sit steadily on his heels, to rise quickly, and to be firm on his feet.

When quite small, the two sexes played together, but the restraints and duties put on girls soon separated them from the boys. When grown, there were few recreations shared in common by the sexes. In olden times, no girl was considered marriageable until she knew how to dress skins, fashion and sew garments, embroider, and cook. Nor was a young man a desirable husband until he had proved his skill as a hunter and shown himself alert and courageous.

Politeness was observed in the family as well as in the presence of strangers. The etiquette in reference to the fire was always observed (children didn't walk in front of adults), and care was taken not to interrupt a speaker, and never to accept anything from another without recognition by the use of an expression the equivalent of "thank you."

LEARNING FROM MOTHER: In the past, when life was much more simple and the people followed lifelong routines, Native children learned their cultures and traditions by direct daily participation. Even in the 1920s, when this photograph was taken on the Southern Cheyenne Reservation in Oklahoma, little girls had lots of time and desire to learn their tribal ways from family elders, especially their mothers and grandmothers.

Here is young Nellie Runs Between, spending time with her mother, Mrs. Runs Between, whose maiden name was Kills Enemy. The two are wearing matching dresses of heavy trade clothe decorated by rows of cowrie shells brought by trade from the Pacific Ocean to the Plains. Although fancy dresses like these were saved for special times—and were worn here for this photo—the women and girls of many tribes still dressed quite traditionally in the 1920s, even as the boys and men pretty well all wore store-bought jeans, shirts, and shoes.

Education among the Flathead-Salish

(Harry Holbert Turney-High, *The Flathead Indians of Montana*)

Flathead did not take the prepubertal education of children very seriously. The father was bound to provide for his offspring, and his wife to be responsible for their conditioning into the tribal mores. He also gave a certain amount of desultory economic instruction to his sons, as the mother did to the daughters. Before puberty this was mostly by example and emulation. Children were urged to be helpful and to be anxious to learn. Informants say this urging was seldom necessary for "we were anxious to please our parents in those days and to get their praise. We were proudest when we could surprise them with something extra we had done." Informants say that children in the old days were not actually required to work. In all the above, the father was glad to receive the advice of his/or his wife's brothers.

The foregoing statement indicates a bilateral family, which apparently is the correct assumption. However, as stated before, children were considered primarily members of their mother's family, and for this reason the maternal uncle took far more interest in their well-being and deportment.

Certainly this education of the child was entirely a family matter. No council or chief ever appointed some wise and experienced old man to take charge of boy-training. The afore-mentioned child-policeman was not given this burden. However, it is possible that more people took a hand in the control of the child than on the Plains. Aside from his parents, he felt the influence of the grandparents strongly. Then the burden of the avunculate fell upon him, as well as the continual correction of the aunts, who referred to the children by the same terms as they spoke of their own offspring. Later we shall see that elder first cousins made themselves tyrants of no mean proportions. Furthermore, the younger children were under the constant supervision and reproof of the elder ones. The first born son or daughter had authority over the subsequent ones throughout life.

There was much time for play, and children had several games. Little girls were fond of their dolls. These were made by their mothers while they were little, but big girls were proud of their skill in fashioning their own dolls. The material was of buckskin and later of fabric. Clever women made quite lovely dolls for their little girls, going to some length in painting the face and making buckskin clothing for them. Little girls played with their dolls until puberty, and sometimes after that. A common rebuff to a lovesick swain was, "I like playing with my dolls and don't want you to give me a real one." Not infrequently a girl took her dolls into the lodge when she married and kept them for life.

Children were not allowed to romp in the lodge, especially near the backrest tripod where the medicine bundle and weapons were. They were put to bed with the dark. Therefore, if children refrained from sexual precocity, were seen rather than heard, kept away from sacred objects, and obeyed promptly without too much show of petulance, if they were helpful to elderly people who might pray for them, they were accounted "good children."

PUBERTY

The Flathead had various names to apply to girls at certain ages: a toddler, a girl large enough to perform light tasks, a girl of about twelve, and a girl after puberty. These terms do not represent age societies or any other formalized age grouping, a concept foreign to Flathead social organization.

Now when the mother thought that her daughter might be approaching puberty, she took the girl aside and warned her. Of course the girl was well aware of the ordinary fact of sex. The crowded lodges took care of that. But the daughter was warned about menstruation and carefully enjoined to tell the mother as soon as the first signs appeared.

Female informants today vigorously deny that a girl had to leave the lodge and live alone at her first menses. They also deny that this was done at any subsequent menstruation. They ridicule the Snake for thinking that such feminine blood was bad medicine. In any event, as soon as the mother ascertained that the girl was menstruous, she sought out a wise old woman to become the daughter's guardian and instructor during a four-day period which was to follow. Great care was exercised in this choice, as the young woman was thought to become like her elderly mentor in chastity, industry, skill, capacity, and even in ease of childbirth and fecundity. A bond was established between them for life so that the younger woman felt obliged to aid the elder until death.

This crisis period was singularly lacking in ceremonial, but was rigorous enough to demark adolescence from childhood with great clarity. When an old and circumspect woman, preferably from the family connection, had been found who would undertake the responsibility, the dame made the girl take a bath in cold running water. This was necessary even though the ice had to be broken. This initial cold bath was to make the maiden strong and to increase her intelligence. This procedure was to be followed by a woman until the menopause. During this bath the girl was to put much water on her head which would make her hair grow long and lustrous.

Upon the girl's return she was taken to the old woman's lodge where she was to live during the four-day period of instruction. The two then sat down while the elder painted the maiden's face, advising her all the while to adopt a life of sobriety and industry, frugality and obedience. The girl was then ordered to get a rock. With this she was to pound her feet so that they would not get any larger. Flathead did not admire large feet, so that the girl was cautioned not to warm her feet at the fire, but to do so with a hot stone lest her feet assume unfeminine proportions.

She was then told, "pick your lice; get a big one." She then found a large louse and stuck it through with a pine needle. The impaled louse was then placed near the fire and slowly roasted. This was done so that the girl would never be afflicted with lice. The maiden was then sent to bring four loads of fire-wood, a procedure to be followed each morning and evening during this first menstrual period.

From this supply some person from each lodge in camp took a share wherewith to kindle the morning fire.

After she had built the fire at her own lodge she went for a supply of water. From this she must give a drink to all the elderly of the camp who would make a prayer for her. Sloe must not drink of the water herself.

This act of respect accomplished, she fetched the water supply for her own lodge, taking care to empty any stale water remaining from the previous day. She then prepared breakfast for her own parents. At the time of the first period she was expected to do all the family cooking without assistance from anyone, although she could eat none of this food herself. Her own meals were taken in her guardian's lodge.

This work procedure was followed every morning of the period. She must be up betimes while others slept. When she had finished she went to her instructor's lodge where the latter would paint her face while she gave her good advice. All of the girl's toilet was in this woman's charge. Combing a woman's hair always had a certain ceremonial nature among the Flathead. The girl did not wear any special costume during this time.

Throughout the period she was given all kinds of tasks. Orders were peremptory and obedience immediate. The teacher saw to it that her waking day was extremely full and industrious. All this was done for preventive measures as every bad habit a young woman could have was apt to settle in her person at this critical time. In order to circumvent this the girl must continually apply herself to the opposites of such vices so that she might never be afflicted with them in adulthood.

From this time onward the parents exercised every precaution to see that their daughter remained chaste, while the young men used every means open to them to see that they failed. Virgins were highly respected among the Flathead, but old male informants relate that they were rare indeed. While no precise set of tabus was set up between an adolescent girl and her brothers, they were never allowed to romp and play together.

BIG BROTHER—LITTLE BROTHER: Siblings of the same sex spent a great deal of time together growing up in tribal life, where school was all around them, all the time. If big brother got dressed up to go dancing, as in this photo on the Umatilla Reservation in Oregon, circa 1915, then little brother got dressed up and went dancing as well. Their clothing includes leather moccasins, cloth leggings with fringed shawl breechcloths, calico shirts, breastplates made of bone hairpipes and beads, along with the feather belts propped up left and right. There is a big round hand drum laying between them, and a porcupine hair roach in front of that, while older brother holds a Winchester lever action rifle.

Ancestral Embers

Parents and children seem to get along well as families when they camp and hike together outdoors. Communication between old and young becomes much easier, away from traffic and TV, sitting together under the shade of big trees, on top of some hill or mountain, or alongside a lulling stream. We hope the stories in this book will inspire those of you with children to go outdoors more often with them. Let your hearts open to each other as they open to the spirits of nature.

Embers from our ancestral past seem to reside within the hearts of everyone. You have probably felt them glowing more strongly when you've gone outside to nature. Can you remember those special feelings you got with your first look at some hidden lake, down into a wild, rugged canyon, or up at a spectacular waterfall? How do you feel when you hear wild geese making their peculiar cries as they fly north or southward across the skies? Children are born to respond to natural environments. We adults need to encourage them to recognize these ancestral embers, while at the same time trying to make them glow stronger within ourselves. What better source of energy could we have for strengthening relationships between youngsters and their moms and dads?

Family life for children back in tribal days meant having many "brothers and sisters," even if they weren't all necessarily siblings. Cousins were called brothers and sisters, as were the children of cousins, and also the cousin's wife's cousins. In addition, non-related lifelong friends called each other brothers and sisters, as did the children of such friends. Perhaps we might put this example to use in these days? Are you willing to discipline yourself to think of close friends and relatives as brothers and sisters, and to treat them accordingly? Are you willing to explain this to your children and encourage them to do the same? Imagine, if we could make this a popular custom!!

Traditionally, little brothers and sisters lived together like a litter of pups, sleeping and nursing together, and often running naked to save wear and tear on clothes in warm weather. But when they got to be about six or seven, their free relationship ended. From there on, it was pretty much intertribal policy to have boys and girls keep separate, except to get married.

One obvious reason for separating boys and girls was to lessen the chances of incest. Another was to keep boys from developing too much interest in the more peaceful pursuits of girls. Homosexual boys were accepted among most tribes—in a few they were even held in mystical esteem—yet parents preferred their sons to grow up as traditional men, able to hunt and fight, and to mate with women in order to have children.

The training of younger children was often carried out by the older ones. Children learned to respect those who were older than they, even if only by a few seasons. This kind of respect is still very evident in many Indian tribes today. We think it would benefit young and old alike if other youths could learn this example from tribal life.

Childhood among the Plains Cree

(David G. Mandelbaum, *The Plains Cree*)

Children wore little or no clothing. Boys ran about naked until they were about five years old, when they were given a breechcloth. At the same age girls were dressed in garments similar to those worn by adult women. During a rainstorm children were stripped and sent out to get wet. Whenever the band camped along a river, the children sent much of their time swimming. They soon learned to use the dog paddle stroke and to float on their backs. The best swimmers among them swam with an over-arm stroke.

They were never beaten and rarely reprimanded. One informant related that as a child he habitually threw himself on his back and yelled if he disliked his foe. The habit was broken when his parents placed a vessel full of water behind him. As he went over on his back, he got wet and when everyone laughed he also laughed.

Even during the most sacred rites children were accorded perfect liberty. An extract from a journal relating to a Sun dance witnessed in 1935 reads: "A youngster, a little over two years old, came wandering into the Sun dance lodge. He stopped near the circle of singers and stood there for fully fifteen minutes gazing abut him. He sucked his thumb for part of the time and was quite stolid throughout the period. Four drums were pounding away a few feet from him and some twenty dancers bobbing and piping.

"Children often wandered in and out of the lodge. At one time during the dance, two boys of about four engaged in a battle, throwing stones and chips at each other. One would run up and pound his adversary with a twig at intervals. I was a bit perturbed, being in the line of fire. But no one else seemed to care; eventually the boys ran out to play elsewhere."

Children spent a great deal of time with their grandparents and relatively little with their parents who were preoccupied with adult tasks and cares. Once, in telling how the souls of the dead sometimes visit the earth, Fine-day incidentally said, "The old people come back to see their children and especially their grandchildren, for the Cree love their grandchildren even more than their own children." When asked for an explanation, he replied that when a person grows old he has more time to spend with the children and so grows very fond of them.

Sex knowledge was not formally imparted, but was acquired by boys and girls largely through observation and the talk of their contemporaries. A boy often attached himself to a young man who was a good hunter and a brave warrior. The two were constant companions and called each other *niwtcewahan*, "he with whom I go about." The young man taught the boy how to hunt and fight and was proud of his protege, since the boy's attentions symbolized his own merit.

When there was a large encampment, boys of different band divisions would play together and become close friends. When camp was broken, one of the boys might go off with his friend's family. After a time the two would go to live with the other household. The boys exchanged gifts and each received many things from the other's parents. If one died, the parents of the surviving boy sent him to live with the parents of his deceased friend for a while. The boy considered both households equally his own. When two such friends grew up and went on the warpath, they shared all dangers. If one were killed, the other was also usually killed. The relationship term they used was the same as that given above, niwtcewahan.

PUBERTY AND WOMEN'S OBSERVANCES

Girls were secluded for four nights at their first menstruation. A small tipi was set up at some distance from the encampment and there the girl remained with an old woman. The pubescent was kept busy chopping wood, sewing, and repairing hides. At night, the old woman would tell her tales and perhaps relate some didactic anecdotes concerning sexual matters. Before the girl was allowed to step out of the tipi the old woman made sure that no men were in the vicinity, for should she look on a man, he would be liable to lose his supernatural guardians. The girl used a minted wooden stick to scratch her head. During her seclusion, she was given very little food to eat and was expected to cry a good deal. This four-day period was regarded as the most auspicious time in a woman's life to receive a vision. Women did not otherwise engage in a vision quest and might experience visions any time.

On the fourth night the women of the camp gathered and went out to the girl's shelter. Four old women who had strong spirit helpers piled up the wood that she chopped and then prayed that girl have a good life. Then they pushed the pile over and each woman carried some of the wood. They led the pubescent to her father's tipi. Four sweetgrass smudges were kindled, two outside the tipi, two inside.

The girl stepped over them one by one; and as she straddled each smudge, the women inside the tipi pray to their spirit helpers. The assembled men and women followed the girl in. A feast was served and the woman who was the leader offered up a pipe to manito and to her own spirits. After the feast, the girl's parents distributed gifts to the guests.

There were no corresponding puberty rites for boys although the vision quest was usually undertaken about the time of puberty.

During menstrual periods a woman slept away from her usual place at her husband's side. She left the tipi only when its cover was painted with a supernatural design. The wives and daughters of men who had important medicine or sacred bundles in or near their tipis slept elsewhere during their menses. The presence of a menstruating woman was believed to defile a religious ceremony and she was forbidden to come in contact with any religious paraphernalia. If a menstruating woman were among the onlookers at any ceremony, the supernatural powers would take offense and bring about an untoward occurrence.

This did not prevent the women from obtaining supernatural powers; and some of the most respected shamans were women. However, they could not lead or vow to conduct certain ceremonies. Thus, a woman who wanted to give a Sun dance would have to induce her husband to make the vow. If she had been given a song in a vision, she taught it to her son or her husband and he would sing it to her during the ritual. Women had no officially recognized voice in political and social affairs.

Gros Ventres Childhood

(Regina Flannery, *The Gros Ventres of Montana, Part 1, Social Life*)

In the days before the buffalo disappeared and before formal schooling was available, childhood, it was said, for girls was shorter and for boys was longer than at present. A girl was ordinarily given in marriage before she was twelve years old, certainly before she attained physiological maturity. A boy on the other hand, though seemingly anxious to participate in hunting and in war as soon as he was able, was not forced to bear the full responsibilities of adulthood until the end of adolescence. While there was considerable variation from family to family in the amount of time required of children in training for practical tasks, all enjoyed a considerable amount of free time.

PLAY

Singer and Coming Daylight, the two oldest of our informants, in recalling the amusements and pastimes of their youth, decided that sliding down hills was one of the most pleasurable as it could be done at any time of the year. In winter, when there was snow, the boys used a kind of sled made by lashing buffalo rib-bones together. Girls managed just as well by simply sitting on their robes and holding between their legs the end which usually hung free. In summer a stiff buffalo hide was used for sliding down the grassy slopes. When the water was frozen, boys and girls alike skated with their feet on the ice, thus clearing a slick surface on which to spin their tops made of horn.

Swimming, however, was the great sport in summer. Girls left their dresses close to the bank, those of the older girls in a neat row closest to the edge and those of the smaller girls in the next row. Beginners used the dog-paddle, but the boys developed proficiency with the overhand stroke and girls with the breast stroke.

Sometimes the children amused themselves by rolling down the bank so that their bodies made a loud smack as they hit the water. At other times they held contests to see who could dive and stay under the longest time, or who could make the biggest bubble by exhaling under water. Follow-the-leader was played even in big rivers like the Missouri, but only the more courageous participated in this game. The one who had the reputation as bravest was the leader, and Coming Daylight claimed that she, herself, often led, one of her accomplishments being the ability to swim quite far under water.

There was no adult supervision of children at play and they spent much time at the water's edge, even when not intending to swim. Modeling in clay was done by boys as well as by girls. The latter liked especially to form wet clay into "parflesches" and incise marks to represent beaded and painted designs.

Walking on stilts, teetering on logs, swinging by standing in a loop of rawhide, all were considered enjoyable activities for little girls. Nevertheless some of their games were quite rough-and-tumble. In one such game, girls formed a circle, each pinching the flesh on the back of her neighbor's left hand; while standing thus they sang a song which was repeated as many times as necessary until someone let go of her neighbor's hand; whereupon this girl was jumped on and mauled by all the others. In another game, one girl, with her eyes closed, would try to find the others who were seated in a row on the ground. Different ones would call out : "This way! This way!" Each was anxious to be the first discovered. As soon as the girl who was "it" touched one of the others, she picked her up and, carrying her upside-down on her back to the spot from which she had originally started, she dumped her burden on the ground. This procedure was repeated until "it" had carried each girl, but the last one to be dumped was tickled unmercifully by all the others.

Girls played with two kinds of balls. One type was of buckskin stuffed with deer-hair. This they would toss to one another. The other type of ball was large and made from the bladder of a buffalo cow, dried and stuffed. This type they would bounce and kick. A popular game played among girls in spring was as follows. The girls holding hands formed a big ring. One girl in the center would have a ball. She would throw it at anyone in the ring. When she hit her chosen victim on the chest with the ball, the girls let go of each other's hands and each ran for a piece of buffalo chip where she would be "safe."

A game played by boys and girls together in the evening was as follows. The children would line up according to size behind the tallest boy who would have in his hand a stick which was smoldering at the end. Each child held on tightly to the one in front of him. The boy holding the stick would try to touch the smallest child at the end of the line. The line would writhe as big sparks would fly and sometimes hair got singed. One old woman, recalling this game, remarked: "I don't know when we would get to bed, we had such a good time!"

Sometimes the children would send one of the group on an errand. Those who stayed behind would wet their hands with their tongues and say: "We will watch this to see if it takes you a long time or not." If their hands were still wet when the member of the group returned, they decided that he had done the errand very quickly.

When there were pretty clouds in the sky a little girl might point one out to the other children and tell them to watch it. Then she would stand at the bank of the river, bending over at the waist and violently swinging her arms from side to side while singing. The others would watch the cloud and tell her that it was disappearing and soon it would be gone. "They used to think they could make the cloud disappear by singing that song."

If a group of girls were playing together and some one boy, say from seven to nine years old, would butt in, the girls would all sit down to show that they resented the intrusion. If the boy did not leave, the girls would then form a circle around him and sing a derisive song. Thus the boy would be shamed and run home. The opportunity for this did not occur very often, since boys from about the age of seven usually went off to be by themselves at play. It was said that a girl, of course, would never think of attempting to break into a group of boys.

Sometimes a group of boys tried to break up the girls' play. One way they pestered them was to wait until they were about to slide down a hill. Just as a girl would be ready to start, one of the boys would grab one of her legs and spin her around so that she would go down the hill backwards.

A favorite sport among boys involved skill in shooting arrows. One game was to plant a marked arrow as a target. Then two boys would shoot two arrows each, and the one whose arrow came closest to the marker would take the arrows of his opponent. Sometimes they would see who could shoot the greatest distance. An interesting variation was to fasten a bow to upright sticks, one stick shorter than the other, so that the bow slanted with the string up. The player would stand on one side of the bow and tap the arrow against the bowstring to get the string vibrating, and when he judged the vibration sufficient to send the arrow toward the marker about 35-40 feet distant, he would release the arrow. Then another player would try his luck. The one who came closer to the marker would take the arrow of the one who lost.

Boys played a variant of the hoop and pole game. The hoop was larger than that used in the game as played by adults and a split stick was used as lance. The thrower aimed at the center of the wheel and, if he hit it, the shot was called "the crow." Another wheel game played by boys was rolling hoops made of green willow wrapped with willow bark. There were no crosspieces in this wheel which was about 16 inches in diameter. Two teams lined up and the hoop was rolled as swiftly as possible by a member of one team while the members of the opposing team by shooting arrows tried to hit the rim of the hoop. If one succeeded and thus stopped the wheel, he retrieved his arrow, placed the hoop against a rock and had a chance to hit the rim while the hoop was at rest.

Occasionally girls, or sometimes boys and girls together, formed a group in the evening to sing in front of the lodge of a rich family who they knew had such a specially loved child. The group danced and sang and then the woman of the lodge would invite them in. She would feed them and say that she was doing so in the name of that beloved child. Coming Daylight described how she joined groups who were going around the comp circle singing in front of the lodges of those who had returned successfully from a war party. This was before she was married and so she had to get permission from her grandmother. Mounted on a horse with a girl friend her own age, whose brother was supposed to keep an eye on them, they rode with the others. Singer admitted she had not participated in such singing parties when she was a child because she never had a horse to ride upon.

Much of the leisure time of children was seemingly spent in play which reflected the daily routine of adult life as well as many aspects of the life cycle. A group went quite far outside the camp circle, for instance, to play they were "married folk." If little boys went along with the girls, some would be "husbands," some "sons," and "sons-in-law." The "women" would tell their husbands, "Go out and hunt buffalo." The boys would go off and stay a little while and on their way back made noises like neighing horses. This would be a sign for the girls to come meet them and make comments such as: "Oh what a lot of meat you are bringing!" Then they would pretend to slice, cook, and eat this imaginary meat. Once in a while the children actually snared a gopher, the skin of which served very well in their play as a food sack.

In order to lend excitement to this kind of play, they might divide into two groups and one "tribe" would attack the other. When their "husbands" or loved ones were "killed," the girls mourned, crying just as they had observed grown-ups do, even going so far as to make marks on their legs with mud to represent cuts. A "corpse" would be prepared for burial, as they had seen the dead wrapped, with the exception that in play they failed to wrap the head. Sometimes girls would take the foreleg of a buffalo, for example, and wrap it up to serve as a "baby." After having gotten from the river a certain kind of reed to serve as their hair, when the baby "died" they cut off their "hair" as a sign of mourning.

Many women described the lodges they, as children, built which were large enough to play in. Garter Snake used a big yellow dog that belonged to her grandmother as a horse, and when her lodge moved she packed everything on travois which dog drew. When it was not convenient to have the lodges built large enough to actually accommodate the children inside, the formation of the camp circle was copied by making large leaves into the shape of tipis. Sticks then rep-resented horses and other sticks attached thereto were travois. These little wooden horses might be fitted out like real ones, with miniature beaded horse blankets, and so on. Occasionally, too, a little boy might pretend he was a horse and drag the travois while being led by a girl as he held a line in his mouth. When this type of horse was out graz-ing, the owner would have a difficult time catching it.

Sometimes the girls pretended that they cut off their little fingers as a sacrifice, even holding sage to the "wound" as in real life. Coming Daylight and Garter Snake, both of whom as children were associated with one of the Sacred Pipes, mentioned that many girls liked to pre-tend that they had one of these Pipes at their play-lodge. They used a certain kind of flower to represent the Pipe and would put it outside the play-lodge in the same position as the real Pipe was placed. They smudged and sang Pipe songs just as their elders did.

Once in a while they would pretend they were going to transfer the Pipe. Mud was smeared on their foreheads just as the Keeper used paint. The others would seize the new "Keeper,'" paint him, go through an imitation of the ceremonies, sing songs, and so on. At the end of the game, however, the rest of the children finally took the "Keeper" and dumped him in the water head foremost, an indignity that would have been out of the question in regard to a real Keeper.

Thus it was evident how much children learned by observation. It was specifically stated in regard to the learning of songs that no one ever sat down with a child to teach him a special song or dance, that he would pick up songs and dances by hearing and seeing them per-formed at the various ceremonies.

Similarly, according to both Coming Daylight and to Singer, there was no special teaching in regard to a knowledge of the Supreme Being. Children would know about Him because they would from infancy have heard older people mention Him. In the old days people never did anything without first saying a prayer. The prayers always started out by mentioning the name of the "One above the White Man" and then names of other beings followed.

BEST-DRESSED AT THE SHOW: Young native people nowadays often wonder why the generations ahead of them nearly lost their tribal cultures, and this photograph shows one answer. It was long assumed by governments, and by society in general, that North American Indians were "dying out," the only hope for survival being their complete integration into Western society. Some tribes felt this pressure as early as the 1600 and 1700s, while others didn't get government agents and church missionaries until the later 1800s. By 1916, when this photograph was taken, the children of all tribes were forced to attend schools where, interwoven with other lessons, were strong messages that tribal ways were "heathen" and bad; that languages and customs should be forgotten and must not be used at the schools, and that signs of modern progress would be much more accepted. Therefore, at the "Indian Baby Show" held in Bishop, California in 1916, the "Best-Dressed" prize went to the Paiute baby who most looked like its European-American neighbors and not to a baby in beadwork and buckskin clothes.

TRAINING

Formal training, in skills necessary for women's work, was begun for little girls at an early age. This was usually in the hands of a female relative-a grandmother or perhaps a widowed aunt-to whom the child would be sent at about the age of seven years. The reason for removing a girl from her immediate family circle was said to have been to protect her virginity. Her parents wanted to send her "where no men were living, as they didn't want a girl around home with her father, brother, male cousins." Should there not be a suitable relative, however, the girls' parents would keep her at home and she would receive training in domestic duties from her own mother. In any case, the girl was supposed to be watched over and kept under close supervision. For her there was much less freedom than for a boy of like age.

So far as training in domestic tasks is concerned, it was considered an important part of a girl's duty to gather berries and to dig roots. Some older woman went with a group of girls to show them what to collect, pointing out at the same time the things that were not edible. Each girl worked and whatever she garnered would be given by her to her mother or grandmother. What was not used immediately would then be stored for winter use.

Learning to slice meat very thin for drying seemed to have been picked up easily by girls at playing "house." Skinning and butchering were much more difficult asks which had to be learned carefully. These were considered mainly work for men, but it was useful if a woman knew how to do them, and only those who had mastered these skills were taken on hunting parties. Coming Daylight acquired this type of knowledge only after she was married, at which time she was only about eleven or twelve years old, and before she had borne any children. She gradually learned the names for each cut of meat and the certain ways of butchering each type of animal.

There were individual differences in the kinds and amount of work which a girl would learn. Some were more proficient than others, due mainly it would seem to the type of training received. Coming Daylight was an orphan and was raised by an extremely strict maternal grandmother, who made her stay by her side for hours as she worked along with her, correcting her mistakes and demonstrating the proper ways of doing things. Coming Daylight heard the other girls and boys outside playing and would sometimes cry because she had to learn a woman's work instead of joining in the fun. Singer, although raised by a grandmother, was allowed to play out much more than was Coming Daylight, and admittedly never mastered as many techniques as the latter. Garter Snake, who was chosen by her parents as Pipe Child when her father was Keeper of the Feathered Pipe, was well-trained by her mother, but apparently did not begin formal instruction at such an early age as did Coming Daylight.

Regardless of individual differences, however, one of the first acquired and most essential tasks was that of working hides. The next step was learning how to scrape buffalo hides. Apparently all women knew how to do this and, in the times before the buffalo disappeared, were kept constantly busy at it. After becoming proficient at scraping, the next process learned was that of tanning. There were various ways of preparing hides depending on the different uses to which they would be put, whether for lodge covers, clothing, harnesses, and so on. Then came the important steps of cutting out and of sewing. Usually girls began by cutting out moccasins and finishing them off. Later came dresses and leggings. Knowing how to make parfheshes and to paint them was likewise considered an essential part of this early training for girls. It was only considerably later that the ability to put together a lodge covering of buffalo skins was acquired. This was considered the most difficult of all tasks allotted to women and not everyone was able to do it.

The whole training of the girl was oriented toward marriage. A girl was supposed to have been ignorant in sex matters until informed by an older person, presumably in most cases by a grandmother. Coming Daylight, for example, remembers very distinctly that when she was about ten years old and the man who became her first husband had asked her uncle for her, her grandmother warned her: "Don't be 'ashamed' of your husband." The old woman then told Coming Daylight what to expect as to the physical side of marriage. Her grandmother also told her many other things, as was usual for a girl about to be married. "Now you are going to be married. You be true to your man. If some young fellow comes to you and wants to 'throw in with you,' you tell him no. But refuse him in a nice way and don't say bad things. Try to get out of it nicely. Then go right to your husband and tell him what happened, because if he sees you talking to another man he might get the wrong impression and think you have consented. Moreover, never become jealous of your husband nor should you ever fight back at any woman who might attack you on account of wanting him. Just pity such a woman. Always remember you are the wife; the other woman is not married to him but you are."

All during the time they were learning domestic skills, girls were told that they should keep everything that they own nicely and to have on hand everything they may need. It was not good to run around and borrow. "Keep your house clean and keep everything in good order, then your husband will like to stay at home." Again, "Don't let your husband's moccasins wear out before you make another pair. Always have things prepared ahead of time." Girls were told, too, that good wives took their husband's moccasins off for them when they came home tired, and so on.

Coming Daylight always admonished her daughters: "Never talk back to your husband. Women have fiery tongues when they get mad, and that is bad." It was nearly always taken for granted by others that the wife was to blame if her husband beat her. Since it was customary for very young girls to marry men very much older than they, such husbands took upon themselves the role of disciplinarian.

While marriage was taken for granted, apparently a girl was free to accept or to reject medicine power. Neither girls nor women went on power quests, but some individuals were vouchsafed some kinds of supernatural power in dreams. While the experience of Coming Daylight may be unique, it is illuminating.

"Even before I was married, I had a particular kind of dream which indicated power to extract illness from the body of a patient. This dream occurred four nights in succession. Each morning I would tell my grandmother about it. The old woman got angry each time and told me not to talk about it, to keep it to myself so that I would become a great doctor. But I had already made up my mind that I did not want such power, the immediate reason for my refusal being that I had seen doctors who swallowed what they had sucked from the weak spot in patients whom they cured, and I just couldn't bring myself to have to do likewise."

Although boys had much more freedom than had girls, they too were assigned tasks at a fairly early age. One of the responsibilities of boys was to water the horses during the day. At about the age of fourteen, however, a boy would be required to take the horses out to graze immediately after taking his morning plunge. He would be gone perhaps three or four hours and would eat only after he returned.

The play of younger boys with bow and arrow was training for later life. The older boys accompanied the men on hunting parties and by the time they were about 18 most were skilled hunters. Some families, it was said, took advantage of the fact that a boy would have killed his first big game—antelope, deer, buffalo—by making a feast at which this game was served. On such an occasion the boy stood at the center and gave away property such as horses and blankets provided by his father or uncle, in order to mark the event. This was considered training for the way he should behave in later life in regard to his own property.

Boys were trained in trapping as well as hunting. There were certain songs which were sung by grandparents as the boys danced around in the lodge both before and after trapping. These songs were supposed to bring luck in finding game.

Sometimes when older boys were out taking care of horses, they would band together, daub their faces and bodies with mud as 'war paint,' and make a 'raid' on the camp in order to steal meat which was drying on racks. The women who had worked so hard to prepare the meat got angry and sometimes fought the boys with sticks. Usually, the boys were successful, and would then cook the meat and have a wonderful feasts far outside the camp circle.

Men encouraged their sons to be brave, and a boy would be anxious to go along on a real raiding party just as soon as possible because a young man had no standing until he had risked his life. An adolescent boy who accompanied a war party had to be a man among men. It was a severe ordeal and the older men had no mercy on these youngsters.

Occasionally as training in bravery, the heart of a bear was taken raw and cut into small bits. After calling together the older boys and young men and lining them up, each one in turn was given a bit of the heart dipped in fresh blood and asked: "Well, are you going to have a brave heart?" Some were able to swallow it easily, but others could not stomach it. Those who were able to swallow and retain it were said to be the really brave ones.

It was indicated by many informants that in the old days a man would almost have to have had supernatural powers in order to be outstandingly successful in war or to achieve fame as a medicine man. In fact it was thought that supernatural powers could be helpful in many aspects of life including gambling and love. Guardians, however, used to warn the boys and young men under their care that "you can't get something for nothing." By this was meant that a person who accepted supernatural power would not live out his full span of life. Thus, according to The Boy, parents emphasized in training their sons that, rather than going on power quests, they should be ambitious to acquire fame and respect by developing their normal abilities. Nevertheless many sought and obtained supernatural powers, visions apparently often being vouchsafed in youth, although the power might not have been used until later in life. It was believed that those who accepted and used such supernatural powers died prematurely.

METHODS OF INSTRUCTION

Oral instruction, or "lecturing," stands out in the Gros Ventres mind as the most important method of child training. All of our middle-aged and older informants agreed that some relative, often either the mother or the father, lectured their children almost every day, telling them what was right and what was wrong and "how to live." If boys and girls were present together, there were some subjects which could not be touched upon and would be reserved for fathers to speak about to their sons and for mothers to their daughters. The lecturing of the child started when it was an infant and continued until adulthood had been attained. Those charged with the training of children felt it to be a duty. As Coming Daylight put it: "They talked to their children right from the start, and before the babies themselves were able to talk they seemed to understand. Singer remarked that, because modern parents do not talk to infants as the old-fashioned ones used to do, present-day infants do not respond by trying to "talk back." Nowadays, the two old women insisted, even infants pay no attention to instruction, and as for older children, some go so far as to tell their elders to shut up!

Under the old regime, however, a child had to listen, whether he wanted to or not, and he had to retain, at least outwardly, a respectful attitude. Cora, for instance, said that she hated this being talked to. Her father was the one who did the lecturing in her family and he used to require that she stand in one spot and not move "while he preached about being good and the ways of doing everything." Singer and Coming Daylight admitted that it was tiresome for the child to be continuously lectured, but they insisted that this is the best way for children to learn. Children are supposed to really grasp what is being said to them from about the age of four.

Charles Buckman's uncle, who was not a Christian, used to tell him: "You have eyes to see, a heart to think, and ears to hear. Listen to what I will tell you. You are a poor boy. As such, be faithful. Believe in the One Above the White Man. Pray to Him, ask Him to have pity on you and so make you a good man some day. Try to be good to all, especially when you become a man. Be good to the poor, good to the old. Never take anything not belonging to you. Never speak evil of other people. Try to be patient. If a man says anything wrong to you, and hurts your feelings, say nothing because if folks talk back it causes quarreling or fighting, which is not good. If a poor man asks you for anything, if you have it, be ready to hand it over to him. If you see anybody hungry and you have it, feed him. If an old man or woman is in need and wants anything done, do it for him or her. If you do these things, the One Above will have pity on you."

All informants agreed that in addition to having been told to take care of whatever property they might have, they were instructed to regard the property rights of others. It was believed that, though the theft remained undiscovered, the thief would be punished by automatic supernatural sanction. "Something terrible would happen to anybody who stole something."

The usual procedure of careful parents when a child reported he had found some article was to first question him as to whether or not he had taken it from someone. Then the parent would go around and ask people if they had lost this certain article. If a child had stolen it he would thus be found out and it was believed that he would never steal anything again.

The rights of children to their own property were recognized by elders and, while they admonished children to take good care of their things, if a child wished to dispose of what belonged to him no one would reprimand him for having done so. After all, generosity is a trait that was much admired among the Gros Ventres. Informants said that if, for instance, a man had given a horse to his daughter and she gave it away, he would say nothing to her about it. Should she ask him for another he might, however, tell her: "Well, I don't know; you might give it away." But he would never scold her about it.

Even if a child were flagrantly disobedient he would ordinarily be punished only by a scolding rather than by whipping or deprivation. Singer and Coming Daylight both were shocked at the idea that a child might be punished by depriving him of something. They said: "Indians love their children and we don't think they would deprive them of anything. They just talk to their children and tell them what is right."

Coming Daylight gave an account of an occasion on which she was disobedient. "One of my relatives was very ill and my grandmother thought that if I would sacrifice a finger joint, he would get well. But I was a small girl and I dreaded the idea of having part of my finger cut off, so I ran away. My uncle chased after me and told me never to come back. I yelled at him: "I won't come back, but I am not going to have my finger cut off!" So I went far off and stayed out in the hills until my uncle came looking for me and brought me home again. Two nights after they had asked me to give up my finger, the relative died, but they didn't punish me."

If a child were really lazy or "pouted too much" he might be "thrown out"—cases were mentioned where this had actually happened. The theory was that the child would then have to work much harder than he would have at home for whoever would take him in. In the case of temper tantrums on the part of a very young child, he was first simply told to stop. Should he continue, his guardian would say: "Oh well, he doesn't know any better" and then douse him with cold water. It was said that he would get up immediately after that type of treatment, and would soon be cured.

If a child were naughty or made a mistake, his guardian would usually not reprimand him in public. He would wait for an opportunity to get him alone. As an example, in training for proper attitudes and behavior between brother and sister, the boy was told: "Be careful what you say in front of your sister." If the boy then made some remark he should not have made in the presence of his sister, his mother waited until the sister had gone out and then talked to him in a gentle way. Cora expanded on this by stating: "The Gros Ventres never bawl out anybody in front of a third party. This is where the white social workers make their biggest mistake. They get everybody together in a central place and then proceed to reprimand the various ones in front of all the others. That is the worst thing that can happen-it hurts these Gros Ventres so badly."

Nevertheless, those in authority may give a severe "tongue lashing" to the culprit in private. As The Boy said when discussing discipline: "The Indian, when he was living the old life, had a system of discipline, but it was not like that of the white man. The Indian used his roaring voice and stinging words. When I was a boy there was one old man who had a crippled hand. On various occasions when we were told to keep quiet and we disregarded that appeal, that old man would sneak up to us and roar at us. Sometimes he would bluff mischievous boys by telling them: 'Come over here. I am going to work you over with this crippled hand,' but nobody would dare go near him. Then he would say: 'Well, give me one arrow apiece. I won't work you over this time-but next time I will surely do so!'

The bugaboo was used to threaten small children when they misbehaved. They were told that someone would come and take them away in a big sack. The story told by Singer and Coming Daylight regarding the bugaboo was that of a woman who put her disobedient son outside her lodge and this "someone" came along with a sack, put the child in it and hung the sack in a tree.

Aside from this bugaboo, Coming Daylight could recall only one instance from her childhood where she was threatened through reference to "spirits." This was after she had swam the whole width of the Missouri River and back. She was, and still is, very proud of this feat, but her grandmother was angry with her for having been too bold in going so far. She scolded her saying: "Why did you do that? Don't you know there are all kinds of animals in the deep water? They always grab what they want!" Sometimes, however, punishment in the form of "something awful will happen" was indicated for the wrongdoer.

One point on which Coming Daylight and the other old women were extremely emphatic was that in the old days the Gros Ventre never tried to scare children by mentioning the Supreme Being in connection with punishment. These old women recalled that in the lectures they heard, and in the scoldings they received, the emphasis was much more on social motivation. Children were told: "Nobody will like you if you do so and so." Or: "People don't like anyone who is ornery. They like those who are generous and kind." Self-regarding motives were stressed in some situations. "Don't gamble lest you lose something we value," "Do what is right so as to keep your man," and so on. In general it would seem that the positive side, rather than the negative, was stressed.

It was more often the men informants who mentioned supernatural motives proposed for proper conduct. They remembered that they were told that the Supreme Being would if have pity on them if they followed the proper code of behavior. Both men and women mentioned, however, that respect for the aged was instilled because "people didn't become old for nothing. They had a blessing from the Supreme Being to live long lives. Whenever you see old people attempting to do something and are having difficulties, you should go right in and do it for them. Help old people out and then ask them to intercede for you that you will have good health, a long life and success in all your undertakings."

The example of others was recognized as effective in child training. Al feels that the Gros Ventres were well brought up in the old days " because children were taught to stick to the rules and they had the good example of adults to follow." In describing the duty of hospitality, Coming Daylight said: "My grandmother was a great one to have a lot of visitors because she was generous, and so I got a good example at home." It was said by others of Coming Daylight: "She feeds everyone who comes along just as she used to see her uncle (mother's brother) do. She takes after her uncle in lots of ways."

In lecturing to the young, examples of actual behavior of persons, both good and bad, were often given. For instance, in warning boys of the evils of gambling, reference would be made to men who would otherwise have had promising careers but who ruined their chances by too heavy stakes which they lost. Fear of offending those who had supernatural power lest they retaliate by means of black magic was implicit in at least some of the admonitions. This was so, for instance, in instructing young men to stay away from the wives of "powerful" men, as well as in warning girls to decline improper proposals in a nice way.

WRAPPED-UP TIGHT: Not even a neck shows, much less the arms, on this little Nez Perce infant of about 1900. The fully-beaded cradleboard top is edged with brass beads and has a laced buckskin bag, part of which is covered with a dark scarf. On the right hangs a little pouch containing medicine to help with daily protection.

THREE INITIATIONS TO TRIBAL MYSTERIES

Above all else, childhood in America's native tribes meant being raised with spirituality. The daily life of tribal children was as filled with religion as that of Amish youths in Pennsylvania or Catholic ones in Rome. Religious rules generally dictated each tribe's dos and don'ts, so these were learned by children right from the start.

However, there is a major difference between the organized religious life of Europeans and the generalized spirituality among America's natives. That difference is perhaps best illustrated by the complete absence in native languages of the word religion. Traditionally speaking, tribal religion was the same as tribal life; the two were not consciously separated.

Instead of written books to give explanations for the universe and its mysteries, native peoples on this continent relied on ritual initiations and endless oral sessions to pass their own tribe's explanations and understandings from one generation to the next. This process began right after birth and lasted through to death. It was part of life for every single native child, just as surely as eating, sleeping, or growing old. In fact, there were prayers for each of these activities, and for nearly everything else in life. There was a continuous acknowledgment of greater Powers, and this gave children an unquestioning, lifelong faith that is virtually impossible to find nowadays in our confusing world.

A native child's first initiation often came within weeks of its birth and involved its receipt of a name. This event is comparable to church baptisms. Native children of modern times often receive both kinds of blessings, their parents finding no conflict between the new and the old.

Children often show their need for wanting "to belong." Initiations and society memberships answered this need within many tribes, some of whom have continued these traditions without interruption, while others have lately tried to revive some of them from the past. It is unfortunate that modern schooling and entertainment have distracted so many children from their traditional ways, even when such were offered to them, although some tribes have been much less affected in this than others.

A Winnebago Boy's Initiation

(Paul Radin, *The Winnebago Tribe*)

I was about thirteen years and over when they told me that they would make me a member of the medicine dance. I liked it very much. Some people do not like it at all when they are asked to join the medicine dance (because of the strict initiations). Very much did my parents desire me to do it. If I wished to live a holy life, that is what I should do, they told me.

This ceremony molded me. I paid the most careful attention to it; I worshiped it in the best way I knew how. I was careful about everything in my life. I never drank liquor. A holy life it was that I sought and most earnestly did I pray that I might live over again. That is what I yearned for. If I do everything that this ceremony enjoins upon me well, I will return to Earthmaker, they told me. This is what I wished. I was doing well as a medicine man and everyone loved me. This ceremony was made with love.

If at any time any of my leaders in the medicine dance wished to give the ceremony I would stay in his house together with those who had been invited. I would do all the work for him, sing the medicine dance songs, etc. All the different things he was supposed to do, all that I would do for him.

When his wife cooked, I carried the water for her, I made the fire, and helped her with the dishes. All the work she liked to have done in the house, I did for her.

All the clothes I possessed I gave to him. Money I gave to him, and the food he needed I procured for him. Whenever he gave a feast, in addition to what he cooked, I would put a special pail of food on the fire for him. When he ate it he was thankful.

One day he said to me, "My son, you have been treating me very well. Even my own brothers never treated me the way you have been doing. I thank you. All my relations hate you, but don't pay any attention to them. You are from a different family and I am teaching you various things, they say. They want me to stop instructing you. My father left the medicine dance for me to take care of. I am in complete control of it. . . . My ancestors would say that you are my relative for what you have done. . . . My knowledge of this ceremony belongs to you, for you have paid for it. My remote ancestors told their descendants, as it has passed down from mouth to mouth to us, that whosoever pays careful attention to all that pertains to this ceremony, that whosoever has a good memory, he is the one to whom it should be taught. Thus they spoke."

Poor Wolf Joins a Hidatsa Boy's Society

(Excerpt from Robert H. Lowie, *Societies of the Hidatsa and Mandan Indians*, American Museum of Natural History, New York, 1913).

When Poor Wolf was seven years old, he joined the Notched Stick society. Together with other boys of about the same age, he bought the privileges of membership from the group of older boys then in possession of them. For twenty nights the buyers were obliged to entertain the sellers. On the twentieth night, a woman was made to stand up by the sellers; she held in her hand a bundle of willow twigs, painted red at the top and enclosing a central stick of greater length, which was spotted in the middle. This woman danced, and the buyers were obliged to pile up property until the heap reached the woman's forehead. The sellers tried to press down the heap of goods, while the buyers tried to swell it as high as possible.

When the pile had reached the required height, the goods were removed, and the process recommenced, until four piles had been accumulated and taken away. The buyers sometimes added a tent (or tipi) in order to increase the height of a pile. Poor Wolf's group was assisted in this purchase by members of some higher group, who considered themselves friends of the buyers. . . .

During the twenty nights preceding the consummation of the purchase, the sellers discussed matters with the buyers, and instructed them about warfare and other all-airs. The final step was taken when each boy, on the last night, approached an individual of the upper grade, thus selecting him for his "father," and presented him, according to his means, with a horse, a gun, or a bonnet. Each novice was free to select whomsoever he pleased for his special father, though the entire group stood in the relationship of sons to the entire group of sellers.

The son approached his father and said, "My father, you must give me a feather to tie to my head." The father, if sufficiently distinguished, might fulfill the request himself otherwise he would call upon a brother of his, who thus addressed the son: "After belonging to the Notched Stick society I did so-and-so (describing a brave deed in battle)." He then tied a feather to the novice's head, told him of a vision received by himself, gave him his own paint, and expressed the hope that the boy would grow up to be an old man and would be successful on the warpath.

At the time of the smallpox (in the mid 1800s), most members of the Notched Stick society died, including Carries-arrows, in whose earthlodge the meetings were held. Poor Wolf's group never sold the membership to a younger generation, hence Poor Wolf, aged 90, still considers himself a member of this society.

Daughters of Ponca Chiefs

(Excerpt from Alanson Skinner, *Ponca Societies and Dances*, American Museum of Natural History, New York, 1915).

One man who had been a brave and had joined many different societies, was working up to the chieftainship, and so, had his daughter tattooed. He prepared a large feast, and got together 100 awls, 100 knives, 100 black silk scarves, 20 or 30 blankets, 2 strands of sleigh bells, and 100 plates. He killed two buffalo and got their grease, prepared two large pipes and two extra ones, with tobacco and kinnikinick, set up a large tipi, and ordered two women to cook the feast. They, of course, had to be dressed well and feasted at his expense. He next asked all the chiefs to fast and tattoo his daughter. The wives of the chiefs and other guests sat in a circle outside the lodge, and were also feasted. Each tattooer received a horse with saddle and bridle.

Sometimes several men joined and all had their daughters tattooed at once. Tattooed women (a small blue mark the size of a dime was made on the forehead, between the eyes) formed a sort of a society, and were privileged alone to wear soft-soled moccasins of a certain type. They were the socially elect of the tribe.

There was great rejoicing, drumming, singing, and dancing at these feasts. After it was over, a herald announced that the giver was half-a-chief. The next step towards the chieftaincy after having one's daughter tattooed, was to have her ears pierced. The chiefs were again called in, and those who did the piercing each received a horse. A feast was given and many blankets distributed.

A Girl Joins a Mandan Women's Society

(Excerpt from Robert H. Lowie, *Societies of the Hidatsa and Mandan Indians*, American Museum of Natural History, New York, 1913)

The White Buffalo Cow society was the highest of the women's societies known to the Mandan and Hidatsa. The leader was an elderly woman wrapped in the skin of a white buffalo cow. Only the older members had the tattoo marks between mouth and chin that were distinctive of the society.

Calf-woman joined the White Buffalo women when she was only two years old. Two years later she began to take part in the performances. Some old women went round the village looking for a female child whose parents loved her dearly and had given away a great deal of property in her honor. They came to Calf-woman's parents, and they consented to have their daughter adopted. Calf-woman's mother gave Brave-woman one pony and several blankets on this occasion. Whenever there was a dance of the society, a member named Berry carried the newly adopted infant on her back. There were about fifty women members, and five men acted as singers. The most important dance, or ceremony, of the society took place once a year, on four successive nights in the winter.

Sometimes the dance was kept up every other night for a month. The object of the ceremony was to lure the buffalo.

Any old member (of the White Buffalo Cow society) could adopt as many new ones as she wished, and was obliged to provide each with a headdress (made from a strip of skunk skin, with feathers attached). Calf-woman obtained one of these headdresses at the time of her adoption, though she was only two years of age. She became a middle officer because her adoptive mother (the old member) gave her the appropriate calfskin robe.

Fasting Customs Among Winnebago Children

(Paul Radin, *The Winnebago Tribe*)

From the age of five, children, male and female, were taught the customs of their ancestors in a series of talks always delivered by an elderly male relative, perhaps the father. The specific training differed, of course, for individual boys and girls. Personal training ceased at the age of puberty, when all of the boys and girls were sent out to fast. For boys, this fasting constituted the only puberty rite. After their faces had been blackened with charcoal, they were sent to some neighboring hill with the injunction not to return till dawn. Gradually, they would be sent out for two, then three, nights. If after that trial they were not blessed, they would be advised either to desist entirely or exhorted to fast until they were blessed, no matter how long the time required to secure the desired result. While fasting, the boys and girls used the following formula (or prayer): "Spirits, am I likely to be blessed? That is why I am praying."

One old Indian informed the author that in former times the young boys and girls were offered either bread or charcoal for their fast. If they took the charcoal, well and good; but if they took the bread, they were unceremoniously kicked out of the house and the charcoal was thrown after them. From other statements of this informant, one might gather that the young generally took the bread.

A faster is always told to be careful as to what kind of spirits bless him, as he might be blessed by a bad spirit. Therefore a faster's blessings are always reviewed by the elders. Old people used to call the children in at dusk, as the evil spirits were said to be around then.

My informant was of the opinion that the parents purposely treated their children roughly, so that they might feel all the more miserable while fasting, and thus pray all the more intensely.

All boys do not seem to have approached the ordeal of fasting with the proper religious feeling. One instance in particular showed anything but a reverent attitude, as told: "When I was a young boy, my folks made me fast together with a boy named Modudjeka. We were supposed to go to the hills and cry until the spirits blessed us. However, whenever we looked at each other and at our charcoal-blackened faces we could not refrain from bursting out laughing. Whenever we made up our minds to cry, something would induce us to look at each other and the laughing would begin all over again. When the time came for our return to the house, we didn't present the slightest indication of having cried, so we took some saliva and made long streaks on our faces."

Omaha Ceremony to Honor a Young Girl

(Information from Alice C. Fletcher and Francis La Flesche, *The Omaha Tribe*, vol. 2, Twenty-seventh Annual Report of the Bureau of Ethnology, Smithsonian Institution, Washington, D.C., 1911)

Omaha families of high standing went through a complex series of ceremonies, including one that brought lifelong honor to a selected girl. Usually this was the eldest daughter of the family, but if they had none, the daughter of a relative or even a close friend was so honored, instead. In either case, she had to be a virgin and recently reached puberty. For her, the high point of the ceremony was a ritual tattooing, by which she was tribally considered to have received the "mark of honor."

The girl was specially dressed for this event in an elaborate outfit made of new, clean leather. Over her dress she wore a soft-tanned robe that was embroidered in colorful, symbolic designs with porcupine quills. Upon entering the ceremonial lodge, which was crowded with notable members of the tribe, the chosen girl was required to perform a sacred dance, which "dramatized the awakening of the feminine element—an awakening everywhere necessary for a fulfillment in tangible form of the life-giving power."

Usually one of the tribe's chiefs performed the tattooing. Among the fees paid by the girl's family for this honor were to be one hundred knives and one hundred awls, considered to be male and female implements, thus adding to the event's symbolism. The work itself was done with the aid of steel needles tied together in a bunch. Small bells were fastened to this bunch to intensify the pain. In earlier days, flint points were used instead of needles, and the rattles of rattlesnakes took the place of bells.

The designs were first traced on the girl's skin with a flattened stick dipped into a solution made from crushed charcoal. After the design was pricked into the skin with the needles, more charcoal was applied. A round spot on the forehead represented the Sun and was always done first. A special song was sung for this. Next, a large, four-pointed star was placed on the girl's chest, again to the tune of a special song.

Other designs used on these occasions included crescents for the Moon, which were placed on the back of a girl's neck, along with turtles, which were put on the backs of the hands. During these proceedings, the chosen girl was expected to make no sound or outcry of pain. If the tattoos healed quickly, this was considered a good omen for her life.

Children of the Iruska

(Excerpt from James R. Murie, *Pawnee Indian Societies*, American Museum of Natural History, New York, 1914)

In this organization there were but six or seven members. They carried quivers full of arrows which were very highly prized, so when an arrow was shot they went to hunt it. They were known as "saaro," youths.

They did things by contraries. If a woman said, "Do not get water," they went after it. They were given to playing the wheel game and because of their peculiarities, no one played with them. If an enemy attacked the village, the members would continue to play the wheel game and pay no attention to the fighting. If a person came up and said, "Do not go out to fight," they rushed out at once. They were always painted black, as if ready to fight. On the head, each wore the skin of a blackbird. The society is said to have been handed down by this bird. The leader so appointed by the bird went through the camp and selected boys who seemed queer, or even insane. These he organized into a society.

Sioux boy and girl in a photography studio.

They did not go into a fight until they were told not to; then they simply shot their arrows toward the enemy without taking much aim and then went to get them; or in other words, an idiotic performance. At all times of their lives they did things in reverse order. They never married or had anything to do with women. Whenever strange or mysterious animals were reported that were feared by other people, they would try to kill them. It is said that the society became extinct by all being killed in a battle except one, who afterwards disappeared.

A Sioux Boy as Heyoka

(Told by Calico, age 68, of the Oglala Sioux, excerpted from Clark Wissler, *Oglala Societies*, American Museum of Natural History, New York, 1916)

One time when I was about 13 years old, in the spring of the year, the sun was low and it threatened rain and thunder, while my people were in a camp of four tipis. I had a dream that my father and our family were sitting together in a tipi when lightning struck into their midst. All were stunned. I was the first to become conscious. A neighbor was shouting out around the camp. I was doubled up when first becoming conscious. It was time to take out the horses, so I took them.

As I was coming to my full senses, I began to realize what had occurred and that I should go through the heyoka ceremony when fully recovered. I heard a herald shouting this about, but am not sure it was real. I knew I was destined to go through the heyoka. I cried some to myself. I told my father I had seen the thunder: "Well, son," he said, "you must go through with it." I was told that I must be a heyoka, and if so, that I would entirely recover. If I did not go through the ceremony, I would be killed by lightning. After this, I realized that I must formally tell in the ceremony exactly what I experienced.

I also saw in the dream a man with hair reaching his heels, while all over his back were many birds moving about. He was painted red, and there were longitudinal marks with forks at the ends on his arms and legs. On his face were live tadpoles and dragon flies. He carried a sinew-backed bow with four red arrows. In one hand, he carried something covered with horse flies, which seemed afterward to be a dew-claw rattle.

In the heyoka, I was ordered to array myself as nearly like this dream man as possible. So I had a long-tailed bonnet made, and covered the tail with feathers. On my face and body I painted tadpoles and dragon flies. In one hand, I carried a dew-claw rattle and a string of the same over my shoulder.

When everything was in readiness, I came out and danced around through the camp with other heyoka, sounding my rattles and dodging about. While this was going on, a cloud came up and threatened rain, but after we stopped it broke away. Then I took off my regalia in the ceremonial tipi, and some old heyoka took the things out to a high hill and left them as an offering. They said I did very well.

After this I did not feel uneasy and afraid because of a threatening storm. Hence, I believed there was much truth in the teachings. This is what one must do. He must make a feast and invite the heyoka. Thus I did. I told them all about my dreams. Then two heyoka took me in-hand, arranged my regalia, gave me instructions and saw me through.

Now, there are two kinds of heyoka. One kind are crazy and foolish. I was of this kind. When they take in new members, they fill a kettle with boiling meat. Then all thrust in their hands to grab for the finest pieces.

They have two kettle bearers to bring the kettle into the ceremonial tipi. The heyoka dance around it, singing heyoka songs. They select roots to chew and rub on their hands and bodies; this is medicine. As the leader sings, all get ready and, baring their arms, crowd up around the kettle, joking with each other. One will dip up water out of the kettle in the hollow of his hand and dash it in the faces of the others. Then they plunge their arms into the kettle and grope around in the soup. I went through with this. The medicine keeps the water from scalding.

Clowns Among the Crow Tribe

(Excerpt from Robert H. Lowie, *Societies of the Crow*, American Museum of Natural History, New York, 1913)

The man who takes the initiative in the arrangement of the perform-ance (of clowns) bids his friends meet in the brush, bringing with them gunnysack, mud, and leaves. They make leggings of gunnysack and one-piece shirts with an opening for the head. Mud is used instead of body-paint. A mask is made out of cloth and blackened with charcoal, with slits cut for the eyes and mouth. The nose is sometimes fashioned out of mud and stuck on, while at other times, it is simply marked with charcoal. When the clowns have disguised themselves so as to be quite irrecognizable, they leave their hiding-place and approach the camp.

As soon as people catch sight of them they cry, "The impersonators are coming!" The clowns walk as if they were lame and act as clumsily as possible, so that the spectators cannot refrain from laughing at them. The people crowd in on the performers to watch their antics. One of the clowns is dressed up as a woman, wearing a fine elk-tooth dress; he is obliged to walk, talk, and sit like a woman, and is stuffed so as to simulate pregnancy. Among the clowns there is a singer who has been provided with a torn drum, the worst that could be found …

The clowns attempt to make fun of anyone they like, regardless of his distinction, because everyone is laughing at them. The spectators try to identify the actors and to inform one another who they are. Then the clowns act like monkeys. They talk to one another in whispers and bid one another dance, so as to make the people laugh. In addressing the crowd, they disguise their voices. As soon as they see the singer pick up his drum, they walk about, preparing to think up some antics. The singer takes up his drum as if to beat it, but merely rattles it, at the same time heaving a grunt. The impatient onlookers cry out, "Dance! We wish to see you dance!"

The clowns have prepared willow bows and arrows, or worthless old firearms, with which to frighten the people while dancing. When starting out on their expedition, they have selected and abducted the ugliest horse, crooked-legged and swollen-kneed, that they could find. Ugly as it is, they have tried hard to enhance its unattractiveness by turning down its ears and tying them with willows, plastering its face with mud or masking it, and putting gunnysack leggings on its legs. Slits are made in the mask for the eyes.

The owner of the horse does not know it has been stolen, until he sees it in the public performance, where it appears ridden by the "woman," who sits behind another clown. This rider with his arrow or gun motions to the spectators, signaling to them not to press too close, but to keep their distance. Usually the people heed these admonitions, which are seconded by the "woman." When the drum is finally beaten, the clowns scatter, each dancing as ludicrously as possible. After a while, the drummer gets excited and throws his drum away on one side and his drumstrick in the opposite direction. He then begins to dance all alone without any music.

When his companions see him acting in this fashion they likewise recommence to dance without drum or chant. Finally, all the performers stop except for one clown, who refuses to cease dancing and thus attracts the attention of the spectators, who cry out, "There's one dancing still!" The other clowns turn around. Then the horseman bids his companion dismount and dance; but "she" refuses and clings to her partner, who becomes enraged and pushes her head, whereupon she gets down and begins to dance. Her companion now makes preparations to dismount, but purposely falls off and pretends to be badly hurt. After a while, he dances with his weapons, then he proceeds to get on horseback again, but intentionally overleaps so as to fall, and again acts as if seriously injured.

Some wags in the audience are in the habit of asking questions and making such remarks as: "These fellows must have come from a great distance." The clowns answer by means of signs that they have come

SHY LITTLE CROW GIRL: Trade cloth dresses decorated with elk teeth were the finest pieces of clothing a girl like this could own, showing that she was from a successful family that cared how its members looked. She also has on a necklace of many strung beads, plus a belt with a long drop, both of which are decorated by conchos made from German silver—a very popular style. She must have been going to a dance, or some other important event, probably with her parents.

from very far indeed, and are tired out as a result of their journey; sometimes they say they have come from the sky. Then someone may ask: "How many nights did it take you to get here?" By way of reply, the clown begins to count up to hundreds and hundreds, and would never stop, were it not for the drummer, who seizes him by the back, saying, "You are mad, you do not know where we have slept." Then he throws him down. The clown pretends to fall head-long, but stops after a while, and begins to laugh. In fact, he pretends to die laughing and kicks his feet up in the air.

Little boys, as well as older ones, crowd about, pelting the performers with dung and trying to identify them. While the outsiders are being held off by the horseman, the clowns make a run for the thickest part of the brush, in order to prevent recognition, doff their costumes, dress in their usual clothes, scatter in all directions, and at last slink back into camp.

In July 1911, a group of young boys dressed up as clowns one afternoon and rode to the dance house, where a performance of the Hot Dance (a popular native dance) was going on. They dismounted, entered, and, to the amusement of the spectators, began to dance.

Hosteen Klah: Boy Medicine Man of the Navajo

(Information from Franc Johnson Newcomb, *Hosteen Klah*, University of Oklahoma Press, Norman, Oklahoma, 1964)

Hosteen Klah was one of the most highly recognized Navajo Indians during his era, which spanned from the late 1860s to 1936. He was considered the most knowledgeable medicine man among his people, having mastered several very complex ceremonials, each one lasting some days and nights. That he learned the first of these before he was even ten years old makes him something of a genius in the culture of his people.

Many boys the age of Hosteen Klah were taken away to U.S. government schools, where they were taught to forget their own culture.

But Klah's family had too much pride in the traditional ways to let him wander away from them. Instead, he became sort of a crutch and right-hand man for an aged uncle who lived in the household, and who happened to be the most noted leader of the Hail Chant, one of the complicated ceremonials—this one for curing certain sicknesses.

The uncle took his young nephew along whenever a family hired him to perform the Hail Chant. He and Klah traveled widely over the desert to reach the various places. Along the way they sought various medicine plants, which the uncle showed the boy how to dig up, store, and prepare for aiding the sick and injured.

After a few years, young Klah was sent south from the land of his people to the Apache—ancient relatives—to one of whom his aunt was married. Her husband was a leader of the Wind Chant, which was similar among both people. The complex ceremony lasted five days and nights, during which the leader had to sing many sacred songs and perform numerous ritual details, all in proper order.

This Wind Chant had to be performed for Hosteen Klah by his Apache uncle after a bad riding accident left the boy with numerous injuries, among them a broken collarbone. During his period of healing, Klah managed to learn the details of this ceremony from his uncle.

While Klah was a helpless invalid from his accident, it was discovered that he was a hermaphrodite. Among his Navajo people, this made him a distinguished person—someone held in awe. He was considered to have been especially honored by the spirits for receiving attributes of both men and women. He was thenceforth expected to master both men's and women's skills, and he did so with perfection. Besides learning the complex ways of being a medicine man, he also gained wide fame as the weaver of very high-quality wool rugs. Many are now prized in the collections of museums.

By the time Hosteen Klah returned from the Apache to his own Navajo people, he was a teenager, and already he had some fame among them for ceremonial knowledge. At home, the uncle who had taught him the Hail Chant was too feeble for ceremony. All he could do was accompany the boy and give him background guidance. By coincidence, the first ceremonial that Klah performed in this way was for a nine-year-old boy, only a few years younger than he.

The Hail Chant was being performed for this boy because he had been struck by lightning while herding the family's sheep. He had managed to get the sheep under a big cedar tree, where they were somewhat protected from the rain and hail. He had then crawled underneath a big ewe in the herd, hoping she would provide him with shelter. But when lightning struck the tree, it knocked him unconscious. He was found by his father, who carried him home. When he finally regained consciousness, the boy could no longer talk.

During the days and nights of this ceremony, Klah had to make seven intricate sand paintings illustrating the various spirits involved in lightning and rain. Each detail had to be done from memory, and absolutely correctly. After the ritual, each painting was destroyed. Parts from medicine bundles were used, in combination with herbs, songs, and prayers. On the final day of the ceremony, the stricken boy stepped through the smoke of herbal incense, then turned to Klah and others of the gathered crowd and said, "l am all right now. Yata-hey!"

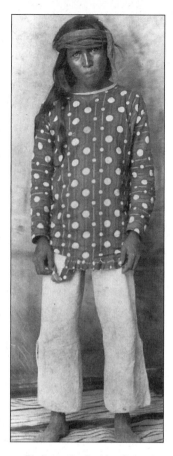

Photograph of a Navajo boy taken about the time Hosteen Klah was this age.

When word of the success reached others in the tribe, the future of Hosteen Klah as a medicine man became assured. There are yet today young Navajo boys who receive ceremonial training from older relatives, like Hosteen Klah from his uncle. To them, he remains the greatest symbol of the ability to find success within their own tribal culture.

FOUR STAYING ALIVE

This is the topic that frightens away the romantics among you, who read the other sections and say, "Gee, it would be nice if we could go back to the old Indian days." The going was tougher then, to put it mildly. Children had to face daily struggles that would put most modern adults under. Imagine sleeping rolled up in a buffalo hide, on frozen prairie ground, at twenty below zero. Then your mom chases you out of bed and tells you to gather lots of wood for the open fire. No matter how much you bring, most of the heat will go up the smoke-hole, and you will never be quite warm enough! And even though your dad's been gone four days and nights hunting, there's still no food. Your mom hopes he didn't get killed by enemies along the way. She boils you broth out of some old rawhide to keep you from starving.

Rugged outdoor life, simple and natural diet, hardiness from cold bathing, these things dictated life for children. Today we can only look for aspects of such a life to try giving our children; it is no longer possible to raise them fully in such ways, even if we choose to try. But read them these stories, ask them if they would not like to go outdoors with you to experience a little something of what they hear about—parents and children just surviving in nature.

My Indian Grandmother

(Excerpts from Charles Alexander Eastman. *Indian Boyhood*, McClure, Phillips & Co., New York, 1902)

As a motherless child, I always regarded my good grandmother as the wisest of guides and the best of protectors. . . .

I distinctly recall one occasion when she took me with her into the woods in search of certain medicinal roots.

"Why do you not use all kinds of roots for medicines?" said I.

"Because," she replied, in her quick, characteristic manner, "the Great Mystery does not will us to find things too easily. In that case, everybody would be a medicine-giver, and Ohiyesa must learn that there are many secrets, which the Great Mystery will disclose only to the most worthy. Only those who seek him fasting and in solitude will receive his signs."

With this and many similar explanations, she wrought in my soul wonderful and lively conceptions of the "Great Mystery" and of the effects of prayer and solitude. I continued my childish questioning.

"But why did you not dig those plants that we saw in the woods, of the same kind that you are digging now?"

"For the same reason that we do not like the berries we find in the shadow of deep woods as well as the ones which grow in sunny places. The latter have more sweetness and favor. Those herbs which have medicinal virtues should be sought in a place that is neither too wet nor too dry, and where they have a generous amount of sunshine to maintain their vigor.

"Someday Ohiyesa will be old enough to know the secrets of medicine; then I will tell him all. But if you should grow up to be a bad man, I must withhold these treasures from you and give them to your brother, for a medicine man must be a good and wise man."

She said these things so thoughtfully and impressively that I cannot but feel and remember them, even to this day.

An Omaha Boy Gets Native Doctoring

(Alice C. Fletcher and Francis La Flesche, *The Omaha Tribe*)

The following was witnessed by La Flesche during his tribal boyhood. One of his playmates was accidentally shot by another young fellow who, with some companions, was firing a pistol at a mark.

After the shooting, the excitement was so intense; and above all the noise could be heard the heartrending wails of the unfortunate man who had wounded the boy in the head. The relatives of the lad were preparing to avenge his death, and those of the man to defend him. I made my way through the crowd, and peering over the shoulders of another boy, I saw on the ground the little form that I recognized. Blood was oozing from a wound in the back of the boy's head and from one under the right eye, near the nose. A man ordered the women to stop wailing and bade the people to stand back. Soon through an opening in the crowd I saw a tall man wrapped up in a buffalo robe come up the hill and pass through the space to where the boy lay. He stooped over the child, felt of his wrist, and then of his heart. "He is alive," the man said. "Set up a tent and take him in."

The little body was lifted on a robe and carried by two men into a large tent that had been hastily erected. Meanwhile, a young man had been sent in all haste to call the buffalo doctors. Soon they were seen galloping over the hill on their horses, one or two at a time, their long hair bowing over their naked backs. They dismounted and one by one entered the tent, where they joined the buffalo doctor who lived nearby and had already been called. A short consultation was held. The sides of the tent were drawn up to let in the fresh air and to permit the people to witness the operation.

All the buffalo medicine men sat around the boy, their eyes gleaming over their wrinkled faces. Then one of the men began in a low voice to tell how in a vision he had seen the buffalo, which had revealed to him the secret of the medicine and taught him the song he must sing when using it. At the end of every sentence, the boy's father thanked him in terms of relationship. Then he compounded the roots he had taken from his skin pouch arid started his song at the top of his voice.

The other doctors, some twenty or more, joined in and sang in unison with a volume that could be heard a mile away. The song was accompanied by a bone whistle, imitating the cry of the eagle. After the doctor had started the song, he put the bits of roots into his mouth, ground them with his teeth, and taking a mouthful of water, he approached the boy bellowing and pawing the earth like an angry buffalo at bay. When near the boy, he drew in a long breath and forced the water from his mouth into the wound with a whizzing noise. The boy spread out his hands and winced, as though he had been struck. The man uttered a series of short exclamations: "Hi! Hi! Hi!" Then the father and the man who had wounded the boy lifted their outspread hands toward the doctor to signify their thanks. During the administration of the medicine, all the men and two women doctors sang with energy (a song), which had been started by the operator.

A second doctor now repeated the treatment and started his song, with all the others joining in the singing as before, while he administered the remedy. At the completion of the song, a third doctor made ready to give his application. (The story continues with each of the doctors taking a turn. One of the songs had words describing the doctoring of a wounded buffalo by its companions at the edge of a pool of water. The buffalo were curing the wound with their saliva, and thus the native doctors were chewing up the herbs and spitting them into the boy's wound.)

The doctors remained all night, applying their medicine and dressing the wound. For four days, the boy was treated in this manner. On the evening of the third day, the doctors said the lad was out of danger; and that in the morning, he would be made to stand and meet the rising sun, and so greet the return of life.

I went to bed early, so as to be up in time to see the ceremony. I was awakened by the sound of the singing, and hurried to the tent. Already a crowd had gathered. There was a mist in the air, as the doctors had foretold there would be; but as the dawn drew near, the fog slowly disappeared, as if to unveil the great red sun that was just visible on the horizon. Slowly, it grew larger and larger.

The boy was gently lifted by two strong men, and when on his feet, was told to take four steps toward the east, while the doctors sang the mystery song that belonged to this stage of the cure. The two men began to count, as the boy feebly attempted to walk, "One, two, three." His steps came slowly, and it did not seem as if he could make the fourth, but he managed to drag his foot and make it. "Four!" cried the men; "It is done." Then the doctors sang the song of triumph.

The fees were then distributed. There were horses, robes, bear-claw necklaces, eagle feathers, embroidered leggings, and other articles of value. Toward these, the relatives of the man who shot the boy contributed largely. One or two doctors remained with the boy for a time. In a month or so, he was back among us, ready to play or to watch another pistol practice by the young men.

FOUR SISTERS: Early reservation life was pretty basic for most of North America's Native People, as seen by this sod-roofed little shack which was home to these four girls and their parents on the Southern Cheyenne Reservation in Oklahoma, around 1910. In spite of their apparent poverty, these girls look happy and neat, wearing the traditional styles then still popular for women of their tribe. Included are long calico dresses, bead-and-tack decorated belts with long drops in front, buckskin moccasins, plus bracelets and strings of beads. The two older girls would care for the younger ones, thus leaving mother to concentrate on the cooking, tanning, and sewing work. If these girls were lucky enough to have mattresses for beds (most likely a single one for the four of them), they were probably on the floor. Early cabin life wasn't much different from how they lived in tipis only a generation or two before.

A Hidatsa Childhood in the 1860s

(Told by Wolf Chief in 1913 and 1918, excerpted from Gilbert L. Wilson, *The Horse and the Dog in Hidatsa Culture*, American Museum Press, New York, 1924)

When I was somewhat past ten years of age, my father took me with him to watch the horses out on the prairie. We watered the herd and about the middle of the day came home for dinner. In the afternoon we again took the herd out to graze. There were many enemies around at the time and we had to guard our horses closely.

While we sat watching the herd, my father said: "These horses are god-like, or mystery beings. They have supernatural power. If one cares for them properly, and seeks good grazing and water for them, they will increase rapidly."

The boys of the household had a strange use for the first dung dropped by a colt. It made an excellent yellow arrow paint. We boys rubbed it on our arrow shafts, or sometimes took it home and rubbed it on our slapsticks, for the game "*umakiheke.*" This quality of the dung continued for the first two or three times a colt dunged. As I recollect, we picked the dung up in the morning and evening. It was a small, gummy mass, about the size of one's thumb. We used it wet; or if it was dry, we spat on it and rubbed the moistened part on the arrow shaft.

My grandfather, Big-cloud, had a fine stallion named Digs-out-dirt, because he always pawed up the dirt with his hoofs when he came to a herd. He was often threatening to the boy herders, putting his ears far back on his head and looking savage, but he never really bit or harmed them. He was a good stallion, forcing his attentions in spite of avoidance and kicks. He raised blue colts.

A colt was broken at two years of age, for a three-year-old is nearly grown, and is then hard to break. Yearlings were sometimes broken, but were apt to develop lameness, or grow knock-kneed from the weight of the boys riding them. The joints of a yearling's legs are still soft. Colts were broken by boys fourteen to seventeen years of age, but boys as young as eleven helped.

As I have often broken colts, I will tell my own experience. Several of us drove a herd down by the Missouri at a place where the current was rather swift, and so likely to prevent a swimming colt from getting back to shore too easily. I roped a two-year-old and drove him into deep water. Swimming out to the colt, I mounted him and made him swim with me on his back.

Now, a two-year-old still suckles his mare. Frightened at my weight, the colt tried to make shore, where he knew his mare was. I clung to his back, forcing him to swim, until reaching shallow water, his feet touched ground and he soon struggled to land. I had dismounted by this time. Following the colt, I drove him again into deep water and repeated the lesson for two or three hours, until the colt was weary. The last time the colt came out, I stayed on his back.

Only one boy mounted a swimming colt, for under the weight of two, a colt would sink. A horse drowns more easily than a man. "If a horse sinks until water runs into his ears, he grows weak," we Indians say.

As the colt reached shore the last time, another boy mounted behind me; and together we rode the poor beast back and forth over the low-lying sandbank covered with soft mud. We rode the colt over such ground until it was utterly exhausted.

Had we tried to mount him when he was fresh, the colt would have bucked and very likely given us a fall. However, in the soft mud or sand, we were not likely to be hurt even if we were thrown off. Certainly, a fall here would not be as dangerous as on hard ground. It was usual for two boys to ride the colt we were breaking, as the animal was thus more rapidly exhausted. We always rode bareback when breaking a colt.

A colt was also taught to swim the Missouri. To train my colt, I needed the help of two other boys. One of these swam ahead with a lariat, one end of which was bound about the colt's head like a halter. I followed, swimming on the downstream side of the colt, guiding him, and clinging with one hand to his mane. A third boy swam at the colt's tail, but not grasping it; now and then he scratched the colt's ham or leg to frighten him and make him swim ahead.

I did not begin to train ponies for war until I was sixteen years old. A boy of fourteen was thought old enough to strike an enemy, and some boys at this age began to train and manage war ponies. A boy as young as eleven might help break colts, but his legs were not strong enough for him to keep his seat on an untrained pony.

A war pony was trained to "dance", as we called it. I took my previously broken two-year-old, mounted, and kicking him with my heels and drawing in my breath with a whistling sound through nearly closed lips, signaled him to go. While doing thus, I also drew on my reins, jerking them repeatedly, as if to stop my pony. Not liking this, he tried to break away, but I checked him each time with the reins, and even struck him (not severely) on breast and fore legs with my quirt. All this made the colt leap and prance about from side-to-side, his forelegs moving together, but his hind legs moving alternately.

I gave my colt several such lessons, in the morning and again in the evening. After two days, the pony had learned what was wanted of him. Every war pony was taught to "dance." In battle, unless a pony was constantly moving, he drew the enemy's fire upon horse and rider alike.

On quiet evenings in summer, a young man painted and dressed in his best, often mounted his trained pony and paraded through the village, making the pony "dance" as he went. Usually just one young man paraded, not several in company; his purpose was to be admired by the village maidens. He wanted them to see what a fine figure he cut on his war pony.

It was the duty of the boys of the household to herd the horses when they were grazing on the prairie or in the hills. We lads, as we guarded the herds, often hunted gophers or blackbirds, which we cooked at a fire and ate. Sometimes we played the arrow-shooting game—two boys shooting against two others, or just one against another. The wager was often a bird or a gopher.

Childhood Quotes

(Excerpt from Gilbert L. Wilson, *Agriculture of the Hidatsa Indians: An Indian Interpretation*, Univ. of Minnesota Studies in the Social Sciences, No. 9, 1977)

Sometimes for fun, we lads used to take long poles with nooses on the end and snare off one ear of a braid of corn as it hung drying, for the braids were soft when fresh. An ear broken off, we would run and make a fire to parch the corn. This was when we were little fellows, ten or eleven years old. The owner would run after us, and if he caught one of us, would whip him. However, this was our custom. The owner and the boy's father looked upon it as a kind of lark, and not anything very serious.

I do not think the younger Indians on this reservation are as good agriculturists as we older members of my tribe were when we were young. I sometimes say to my son, Goodbird: "You young folks, when you want some green corn, open the husk to see if the grain is ripe enough, and thus expose it. I just go out into the field and pluck the ear. When you open an ear and find it too green to pluck, you let it stand on the stalk. Then birds come and eat the exposed kernels, or little brown ants climb the stalk and eat the ear and spoil it." — *Edward Goodbird*

When I was six years old, there were, I think, ten in my father's family, of whom my two grandmothers, my mother, and her three sisters made six. I have said that my mother and her three sisters were wives of Small Ankle, my father.

My father's wives and my two grandmothers, all industrious women, added each year to the area of our field, for our family was growing. At the time our garden reached its maximum size, there were seven boys in the family; three of these died young, but four grew up and brought wives to live in our earth lodge.

When the squashes were brought in from the held, the little girls would go to the pile and pick out squashes that were proper for dolls. I have done so, myself. We used to pick out the long ones that were parti-colored; squashes whose tops were white or yellow and the bottoms of some other color. We put no decorations on these squashes that we had for dolls. Each little girl carried her squash about in her arms and sang for it as for a babe. Often she carried it on her back, in her calf-skin robe.

My father, Small Ankle, liked to garden and often helped his wives. He told me that that was the best way to do. "Whatever you do" he said, "help your wife in all things!" He taught me to clean the garden, to help gather the corn, to hoe, and to rake. — *Buffalo-Bird Woman*

In my tribe in old times, some men helped their wives in the gardens, while others did not. Those who did not talked against those who did, saying, "That man's wife makes him her servant."

And others retorted, "Look, that man puts all the hard work on his wife."

My father said that that man lived best and had plenty to eat who helped his wife. One who did not help his wife was likely to have scanty stores of food. — *Wolf Chief*

The first pots, or kettles, of metal that we Hidatsas got were of yellow tin (brass). The French and the Crees also traded us kettles made of red tin (copper).

As long as we could get our native clay pots, we of my father's family did not use metal pots much, because the metal made the food taste. When I was a little girl, if any of us went to visit another family, and they gave us food cooked in an iron pot, we knew it at once, because we could taste and smell the iron in the food.

Tobacco was cultivated in my tribe only by old men. Our young men did not smoke much; a few did, but most of them used little tobacco, or almost none. They were taught that smoking would injure their lungs and make them short-winded so that they would be poor runners. But when a man got to be about sixty years of age we thought it right for him to smoke as much as he liked. His war days and hunting days were over. Old men smoked quite a good deal. — *Buffalo-Bird Woman*

HOOKING UP THE SNOWSHOES: Outdoor life has always been best taught to children by doing, not by talking about it in a classroom. Our oldest son, Wolf, was about five years old when this photo was taken one snowy morning, as he and I got ready to head across the white landscape surrounding our home to look for fresh tracks and see what animals were coming and going. The snowshoes are laced over our high-topped sheepskin moccasins, their long, webbed shapes letting us walk over the deep snow where our feet otherwise would break through and let us sink to our waists.

Goodbird is Nearly Drowned

(Gilbert L. Wilson, *Agriculture of the Hidatsa Indians: An Indian Interpretation*)

At the mouth of the Little Missouri River, we almost had a fatal accident. When we left our winter camp in the west (in the spring of 1869), the grass was growing and the snow had disappeared, but as we came down the Missouri, a snowstorm came up very suddenly. A strong wind blew; as we rounded the bend at the Little Missouri River, the water was very rough and the waves tossed our boats around so that we were all frightened. Of course, we turned toward shore, both my husband and I paddling vigorously. Usually, in paddling a bullboat (a round, dish-like craft made of willow framing covered by buffalo-bull hides), when a husband and wife are together, the wife kneels in front and paddles, while the husband sits in the tail of the boat to balance it.

Coming down the Missouri, towing a load, was a more difficult operation, so both my husband and I paddled side-by-side in the boat. Suddenly, my husband stopped paddling and leaned over the side of the boat so far that I was nearly pitched over on his side. A bullboat is a clumsy, tub-like craft, and easily upset. My husband leaned over so far that the edge of the boat came clear down on his stomach. "He has dropped the child," I heard him cry, and saw him lift my baby into the boat. "Ina," I cried, but I had presence of mind enough not to drop my paddle. Indeed, we could not have reached shore without our paddles.

As I have already explained, Flies-low, my younger brother, was in the second boat, holding my son, Goodbird. It was customary when a young child cried, to loosen his cradle clothes. After my husband drew the child into the boat, I found that Goodbird's clothes had been so treated. Probably the child had become restless and Flies-low had loosened his clothes a little to give him room to move his limbs. This loosening of the cradle wrapping had made them buoyant, so that the baby floated on the water and my husband was able to rescue him.

Goodbird was crying lustily when we drew him out of the water, but was not choking or strangling. I do not think that his face got into the water at all. I do not remember now whether Flies-low made any outcry when he dropped the infant into the river or not. I did not scold Flies-low. "I am not to blame," he said. "I tried to hold the baby, but that boat seemed to turn upside down and the baby fell out of my arms."

We came ashore without any further mishap and camped in two tents. It began to rain, then the weather turned colder and a heavy snow began to fall and continued for four days. Many of the summer birds had already come north and when the storm was over we found some of them frozen to death.

The Pawnee Girl Who Saved a Prisoner

(James R. Murie, *Pawnee Indian Societies*)

The Pawnee had set out on one of their summer buffalo hunts. Only a few old and sickly people remained in the villages. On the third day of their march they reached the Loupe (River). The main body crossed and pitched camp among the hills, but far behind were a few stragglers and a group of boys playing the hoop game. The latter stopped at the river to finish a game before crossing. Here they were discovered by a Dakota war party and surprised. They scattered out for cover, but a few got away with their horses and crossing the river fled toward the camp of the main body. The whole Dakota party crossed in hot pursuit and were thus led into a trap, for the Pawnee in camp had seen the signals and the whole armed body dashed to the rescue. Many of the Dakota were killed in the running fight that followed.

When the pursuing Pawnee returned, they went over the field to count the dead and collect the spoils. As they were going along, one of the Dakota arose and looked in a bewildered manner; he had only been stunned by the fall of his horse. He was seized and taken to camp. According to custom, he was taken to the chief for instructions. He consulted with the society of braves, then in-charge of the camp, and it was decided to turn him over to the women's society. A messenger was sent to inform the leader of this organization. She at once called in the members, who proceeded to the chief's tipi, marched the prisoner out to the south of the camp, where they bound him to a tree.

The women then returned to the lodge of their leader to prepare their regalia. When all was ready they danced through the village and paraded to the place of torture. Then, as was the custom, they kindled a large fire in front of the prisoner and prepared for a four-day ceremony. Every indignity was offered the unfortunate prisoner. Old women would urinate in bowls and force him to drink. Others would take up coals of fire and touch him here and there.

On the third day, the chief's wife took her little girl out to see the tortures. While they were there, an old woman came up with a bundle. She took out a large piece of dried back fat. This she heated in the fire until hot, and while other women held the prisoner, she spread it on his back. The little girl was overcome at the sight and began to scream. Her mother took her home, but she cried and refused to be comforted.

Finally, the chief asked the cause of this crying, and was informed. He coaxed and threatened without result, for the child declared that she would continue to scream until the prisoner was turned loose. The chief said that could not be done, and so the child continued to wail. The people gathered in and gradually developed sympathy for the child. So the chief called in the braves, but they declared themselves powerless. Then he called in the chiefs and the soldiers to discuss the matter. The sentiment of the camp was now aroused, so four soldiers were sent out to order the women's society to disband. They then conducted the prisoner to the council lodge and seated him there.

The chief then sent for his daughter, who had stopped crying. He stated that they had with some difficulty granted her wish, and that now she must get water for the prisoner. Accordingly, she brought water and held the bowl for him to drink. Then the chief ordered her to get a large bowl of water and some buffalo wool, and when these were brought, to wash the man's wounds. Then, buffalo fat mixed with red earth was given her to rub over him.

"Now," said the chief, "since you would have this man released, you must feed him." So dried meat and fat were brought. Some of the fat she handed to the man to eat, while she cooked the dried meat. When ready, she set the food before him, placed four small bits of meat in his mouth and then signed for him to eat. When he had finished, she set a bowl of water for him to wash. The chief then gave her permission to withdraw.

Then the chief sent for his horses. He ordered his best horse prepared for riding and loaded with baggage for the journey. Next, he brought out clothing and dressed the man in his own fine clothes, even his ceremonial leggings, shirt, and moccasins. Finally, the girl brought a new robe and wrapped it around the man. The chief then addressed the Dakota: "You are to go home. You are a free man. All these things we give you. My daughter here, saved your life. She alone did it. Now go to your people and tell them of her deeds."

Some three years later, the Pawnee were surprised to receive a visit from their enemies, the Dakota. It was a very large party that came to the chief's lodge. The leader asked for the girl who saved the life of a Dakota. Then they knew him. The chief took him into his own lodge and the others were quartered in the village.

The Pawnee entertained their guests well. On the last day, they gave the Iruska dance for their visitors. The Dakota entered into the dance. He was naked; on his body were painted red spots to show his burns and many prints of hands, since he had been held by many of the Pawnee. He addressed the Pawnee, explaining that he had come to see his daughter once more—she who had saved his life—that his own people did not believe his story; hence, he brought them that they might see for themselves. In return, the Pawnee vouched for the narrative.

Many times during his life this Dakota visited the Pawnee, and he labored unceasingly to bring about a permanent peace between them and his people.

Riding a Dog Travois

(Gilbert L. Wilson, *The Horse and the Dog in Hidatsa Culture*)

Small boys sometimes jumped on a dog travois just for the fun of it. Once, I asked my husband to go for wood with me to the timber east of the village. I had three dogs and travois. My son, Goodbird, who was then four or five years old, wanted to go along. My husband and I said, "No, you cannot go." Goodbird wept and wept, so at last we took him with us. As we went along, my little son jumped on and off the travois, walking and riding, and playing with the dogs. The dogs got into a fight and ran off with my little son. He was much frightened, and we laugh about it to this day. — *Buffalo-Bird Woman*

I remember that. There was a road down to the timber, and another road leading to the chokecherry hills that crossed it. We were going along the latter, my father and mother walking ahead, when a woman came down the first road on her way to the village. She had two or three dogs, with travois. Our dogs saw the others and started across the triangle that lay between the two roads. The other dogs turned toward ours, barking. I yelled, "Ai, ai, ai!" I was dreadfully frightened; the dogs were leaping along at such a rate that I was afraid to jump off. The other woman ran between the dogs with her arms up in the air. "Na! Na!" she cried. "Go away! Go away!" That stopped our dogs. I jumped off the travois and ran to my mother. I did not want to ride on that travois again! — *Goodbird*

Games Played by Omaha Children

(Alice C. Fletcher and Francis La Flesche, *The Omaha Tribe*)

In their play, the children were apt to mimic the occupations of their elders. At an early age, the girls began to play "keep house." Miniature tents were set up. The mother's robe or shawl was often seized for a tent cover; the poles were frequently tall sunflower stalks. If the boys were gallant, they would cut the poles for the girls. It was a matter of delight if the tent was large enough to creep into. Generally, the feet and legs would protrude, but if the heads were well under cover, it was easy to "make-believe."

DOG DAYS: Before Europeans brought horses to North America the Native People of all tribes used dogs for packing and working. Children in those times didn't have bikes or scooters, but if they were ambitious they could always train a couple of the family dogs to pull them around. Here are Iniskim and Okan Hungry Wolf as young home-schooled teenagers with their home-made sled and favorite dogs, Baby and Boss, headed down a frozen river channel near their wilderness home in the Canadian Rockies. One of them had to lead the dogs on the outbound journey, but once they were headed back home the dogs could easily pull both boys over the ice at a good clip. It's interesting what traditional fun two boys of the 1980s could still come up with, lacking television and electricity as distractions at home.

Both boys and girls liked to play "going on the hunt." The boys took two parts: sometimes they were hunters, and sometimes ponies. When the latter, the girls tied the tent cover in a bundle and fastened it, and the tent poles, to the boy pony—who might be a docile creature, or a very fractious animal. Sometimes, men carried their pony reputation throughout life. Women would laughingly point out some elderly man and say: "He used to be a very bad pony;" or else, "a very good pony."

The boys who played warrior wore war bonnets made from corn husks, which cost much labor to manufacture and were quite effective when well done. Children made many of their playthings out of clay, and some were very clever in modeling dishes, pipes, dolls, tents, etc.

Dolls were improvised by children from corncobs. Sometimes, mothers made dolls for their little girls, and also small dishes.

The hobby-horse of the boys was a sunflower stalk with one nodding bloom left on the end. Races were run on these "make-believe" ponies. Generally, the boys rode one stalk and trailed two or three others, as "fresh horses."

"The crooked path" was the game familiarly known to us as "follow my leader." The children sang as they ran and made their merry way through the village, each one repeating the pranks of the leader. The line was kept by each boy holding the string about the waist of the boy in front. It is said that the song that accompanied this game had been handed down by generations of children. Certainly, every Omaha seemed to know it.

The quiet games often played about the fire were "cat's cradle" (in Omaha called "the litter"), and a game resembling "jackstraws", in which a bunch of joints of prairie grass was dropped from one's hand, and the players strove to pull out one joint after another without disturbing the bunch. The player could use a joint to disentangle those he was trying to secure.

Another game, called "dua", was played with a long stick, one side of which was notched. The person who could touch the greatest number of notches, saying "dua" at every notch without taking a breath, was winner.

The boys enjoyed a game called "bone slide." Formerly, ribs were used, but sticks are now substituted. Four or five could play at this game. The sticks are about 4½ feet long, made of red willow, and ornamented by banding with bark and then holding them over a fire. The exposed part turns brown, and when the bands are removed the sticks are striped brown and white. Each boy holds a number of sticks and throws one so it will skim or slide along the level ground or the ice. The boy who throws his sticks farthest wins all the sticks; the one who loses is tapped on the head by the winner. The Ponca call this game "arrow throwing."

During the annual buffalo hunt, when the tribe remained in a camp for more than a day, boys ranging from ten to fourteen years of age would . . . arm themselves with sticks about a yard long, to which small twigs were attached. Then, ranging in line through the prairie grass, they scared up the little birds. As these rose, the boys threw their sticks into the air and the fledglings, mistaking them for hawks, tumbled into the grass to hide, only to be caught by the hands of the boys. One lad was chosen to carry the quarry. As soon as the bird was caught, it was killed, scalped, and thrown at the boy appointed to take charge of the game; then it was his duty to run ahead and fall into the grass as if shot. On rising, he took the bird and strung it on his bow string. This little pantomime was enacted with every bird caught. When a number of birds had been captured, the boys retired to a place where they could roast the birds and enjoy a feast. Boys of certain gens (clans) could join in the sport, but could not touch the birds or share in the feast, as small birds were tabu to them.

In winter, the boys played "whip top". They made their own tops out of wood. Sometimes a round-pointed stone served as a top, and was spun on the smooth ice.

A ball game called "ball, to toss by striking," which resembles somewhat the game known as 'shinny', was played by two groups, or parties. This is the game sometimes played between the two divisions of the (Omaha) tribe, which had a cosmic significance in reference to the winds and the earth.

Two stakes, as goals for the two sides, were set at a considerable distance apart. The players with the ball started from the center. The aim of each player was to drive the ball to the goal of his side, while the players on the opposing side tried to prevent this and to drive the ball to their own goal. The bat was a stick that was crooked at one end.

When boy neighbors played together, the "sides" were chosen in the following manner: A boy was selected to choose the sticks. He took a seat on the ground and another boy stood behind him. The standing boy held his hands over the eyes of the seated boy. Then all the sticks were laid in a pile before the latter. He took two sticks, felt them, trying to recognize to what boy they belonged. Then he crossed his hands and laid one stick on one side and the other on the other side of the place where he was sitting. When all the sticks had been taken up and laid on one or the other pile, the standing boy removed his hands and the boy who had chosen sticks indicated to which pile or side he would belong. There were no leaders in the game—the ball was tossed and the sides fell to playing. When men played this game, large stakes were often put up, as garments, robes, horses, bows and arrows, and guns. No stakes were ventured when boys were the players.

Lads sometimes indulged in a game which may be called "dare", consisting of lads doing ridiculous things that required exertion to accomplish. Some of the number were detailed to see that the boys actually did those things that were called for. Many are the laughs the older men have over these "hazing" sports of their youth, as they recount their escapades.

Girls had a game played with two balls tied together and a stick (the obvious symbolism was an accepted part of the game among all the tribes who played it). Two goals were set up several yards apart. The players were divided into two parties, each with its goal. They started in the middle and each side tried to prevent the other's balls from reaching the goal.

Foot racing was another pastime. Races generally took place among the Omaha, however, after a death, when gifts contributed by the family of the deceased youth or maiden were distributed among the successful competitors. At these races, sharp contrasts marked the occasion. The race generally took place a short time after the burial. A feast was given by the parents, after which, if the deceased was a young man, his young male friends took part in the race; if a girl, her young female companions competed for her possessions. The distribution of the goods was made by a personal friend, while the parents often retired to the grave, where the sound of their wailing could be heard above the noise of the contestants.

There was one amusement in which both sexes of all ages, except infants, took great pleasure—this was swimming. The Omaha swam by treading, moving hands and legs like a dog, or by keeping the body horizontal and throwing the arms up and out of the water alternately as the body was propelled by the legs. The people were good swimmers. The current in the Missouri is always strong, so that it requires a good swimmer to make a safe passage across the stream. During the flood season the current is too rapid for anyone to venture to cross the river. Diving was practiced by boys and girls and was enjoyed by men and women, also. In these water sports the sexes did not mingle. Women and girls kept together, apart from the men and boys (this was the case among most, though not all, tribes).

Storytelling was the delight of everyone during the winter evenings. It was then that the old folk drew on their store of memories, myths, fables, and adventures of the pygmies and the "gajazhe" (the little people who play about the woods and prairies, and lead people astray). All these, and also actual occurrences, were recited with varying intonation and illustrative gesture—sometimes interspersed with song—which added to the effect and heightened the spell over the listeners clustered about the blazing fire.

The uncle (the mother's brother), always a privileged character at whose practical jokes no nephew or niece must ever take offense, often

CAMPED AT A POW-WOW: Big enough to sleep our whole family, yet small enough to easily pack into our truck with other camping gear, this canvas tipi was a gift for Okan, whose adopted grandfather, Pat Weaselhead, had already given him an old inherited tribal design to paint on it. This was the first time the tipi had been set up, in late summer of 1981, at a pow-wow held on the small but scenic Eden Valley Reserve that is almost directly east of our family home in British Columbia, with only the massive peaks and dramatic valleys of the Canadian Rockies in between. When our Stoney relatives invited us to their pow-wow, Okan and I decided to walk across the mountains to get there in the manner of the past people. His mom and sister, Star, met us at the camp with our truck, tipi, and other gear. Dressed and ready for the evening dance, Okan was then eight years old and Star was going on three. The announcer told the crowd about our long walk and asked us to do a few rounds of an honor dance, during which many people put money on the floor for us. Said the announcer jokingly, "They don't want you to have to walk back home."

made the evening merry with pranks of all sorts—from the casting of shadow pictures on the wall with his fingers, to improvising dances and various rompings with the little ones.

In the spring, after the thunder had sounded, the boys had a festivity called "striped face", referring to the mask worn by the boys. A dried (buffalo) bladder, with holes cut for the mouth and eyes, was pulled over the head; the bladder was striped lengthwise in black and white, to represent lightning. The boys carried clubs and scattered over the village. Each boy went to the tent of his uncle (his mother's brother) and beat with his club against the tent pole at the door, while he made a growling sound in imitation of thunder. The uncle called out, "What does Striped Face want?" The boy disguised his voice, and said, "I want leggings or moccasins or some other article." Then the uncle called him in and made him a present. Should the uncle refuse to give anything, the boy might punch a hole in the tent or do some other mischief. But generally, the sport ended pleasantly and was greatly enjoyed by old and young.

A Taos Schoolboy at Home for the Summer

(Excerpt from Ann Clark, *Little Boy with Three Names*, Bureau of Indian Affairs, Chilocco, Oklahoma, 1940)

Summer passed slowly in Taos. There were long days and happy star-lit nights. There were days of irrigating. The boys turned the slow-moving water from Mother-ditch into the little ditches to feed the thirsty plants of fields and gardens. Pachole always was patient. He never grew tired of waiting until each plant had its share to drink. He taught Tso'u to think long thoughts while the lazy water moved along, wetting the thirsty earth.

There were days and days of wood gathering. Out-of-door ovens are greedy for the dry branches of the mountain slopes. Pachole taught Tso'u how to tie the sticks into bundles that fit the back with comfort. He taught him how to save his breath in the high places, how to breathe in climbing upward, how to bend his knees in walking down hill. He showed his smaller brother how feet must keep their balance when walking over rolling stones.

The boys dug yucca weed for its fibers. They dug its root for soap. They gathered wild tea and guaco and juniper berries for their mothers to use. They rubbed their faces with the leaves of aspen to keep the wind and sun from burning them. Tso'u helped Iao to dry rose petals. All the Taos girls have pillows stuffed with dried rose petals.

Pachole showed Tso'u the plants that were used for snakebite and for medicines. Pachole knew them all. He was rich in learning.

The boys found the tracks of mountain lion and wildcat. They found a packrat's nest with its sweet little pinon nuts. One noon they rested at the bedded-down place of a bear and her cubs. They saw the deep scratchpads high up on the trunk of a nearby pine tree where the mother bear had sharpened her great claws. They touched the lower scratchpads on the pine tree where the bear cubs had sharpened their little claws.

Once, they saw a deer looking at them through the aspen trees. They smoked a prairie dog family out of its underground hole. They saw an owl on a tree. They shot a chicken hawk, flying.

Pachole taught Tso'u how to use his gun. He taught him how to oil and clean it. Father promised that next summer Tso'u should own a gun. At night Pachole would point out the evening star. He would join in the evening dancing. The old men would listen and nod. Their choice had been wise. They were pleased.

The winds and the shadows, the moon and the stars, were as books to Pachole. He was being taught to read them.

The long days of summer moved slowly.

In the early mornings all the boys of the village ran races. Sometimes they ran in great numbers. Other times, they ran in small groups of three and four. They liked racing.

Tso'u was a swift runner. Pachole could teach him little about running. He ran swiftly and lightly like a young antelope. His feet scarcely touched the ground. "I win all the races," he told his mother. "It is because of the moccasins of deerskin that you made for me. I am a great runner among the boys."

His mother was not pleased with him. "Spend your time in thanking your moccasins," she told him, "and not in bragging." Tso'u went out and sat upon the ladder of his mother's house. He was sorry that his mother had found it wise to scold him.

In the evenings, the people danced. In the houses and in the plaza, they danced. Sometimes the women and girls did the circle dance or the scalp dance, or did dances borrowed from the Plains Indians. The men gathered around them, and sang and beat the drum. Sometimes, the men and boys danced. They danced the fun dances and the dances of the summer season.

Old men taught the young boys the right steps and the words of the songs. Tso'u and Pachole learned the hoop dance. Uncle sang for them. Over and over, they did the hoop dance, for the people liked to watch them.

When the moon was high the young men gathered at the little river that ran through the plaza. The young men of the south plaza stood on the south bank of the little river. The young men of the north plaza stood on the north bank of the little river. They joined their singing. They sang love songs to the girls of the village. They wrapped themselves in their white sheets and sang songs in Taos and in English. They made the music for their singing with their drums.

Sometimes Tso'u and Pachole went with the young men to the little river. They sat on the bridge with the other boys. They must know all the songs when their time came for singing. They wrapped their white sheets about them and learned the words and the music.

Chippewa Government of Children

(Frances Densmore, *Chippewa Customs*)

Throughout the information given by the older Chippewa we note the elements of gentleness and tact, combined with an emphasis on such things as were essential to the well-being of the child. Fear was often used to induce obedience, but not to an extent which injured the child. For example, it was said to be a frequent custom to put a scarecrow where it was unsafe for the children to go. Mrs. English said that she remembered a very steep hill where she and other children liked to play. One day they found a frightful scarecrow at the foot of the hill and they were so scared that they never went there again.

The Chippewa gave much attention to the training of their children. Odinigun said, "In summer the children could play out of doors, but in winter they had to be amused indoors." It was hard to keep the little children quiet in the evening so they would not disturb the older people. The mother often said, "Keep still or the owl will get you." If they did not keep still she went to the door of the wigwam, held back the blanket, and said, "Come in owl, come and get these children, who won't keep still." Then the children put their heads under the bedding and were soon asleep. In the daytime they constantly wanted to run outdoors. Some had no moccasins and were barefoot. The only way to keep them in was to frighten them. So the older people made a birch-bark "mask" of an owl and put it on a stick where the children would see it if they went outdoors. This frightened them and they were glad to stay in. When they were old enough to mind what they were told and to understand things, they were taught that they must not go peeking in the wigwams after dark and that they must not laugh at anything unusual nor show disrespect to older people. They were also taught that they must not go to the neighbors when they were eating and look wistfully at the food. Little children were taught not to go between older people and the fire.

When the children were old enough to listen attentively it was still desired to keep them quiet in the evening. For this purpose the older people devised a game called the "game of silence." In this game a song was sung by an older person in which most novel and interesting events were related. The song suddenly ceased at the most exciting point, and the children tried to avoid making a sound at this surprise. The song was repeated over and over with new words and new pauses, a prize being given to the child who showed the most self-control. It is said that the children were usually asleep when the game ended.

If the children were reluctant to leave their play in the summer evenings a man wearing a mask went among them. He was called the frightener, and the purpose of his visit was to make the children go home and to bed. He wore ragged clothes and walked with a cane. Sometimes his mask was of birch bark that shone with a pale light in the dusk. At other times he wore a horrible mask with a projecting stick for a nose. It was expected that the children would keep still when the frightener came, not bursting into shouts as when they were pursued in the cannibal game. The ability of a child to keep still when surprised or frightened was more important to the Indian than to the white race. For example, the scream of a child might cost the lives of many people if an enemy were approaching the village. When the children went to bed the father or mother told them to lie still and try to think of something nice so they would have good dreams. They were encouraged to remember and relate these childish dreams. There appears to have been a belief that the mind of the child was thus rendered more receptive to the important dream, or vision, that was sought a few years later.

When everyone had retired and the camp was quiet an old man walked around the camp circle, pacing in front of the dark tents. This man was a crier and he made the announcements for the next day, telling whether the people would go hunting or what would be done in the camp. He also gave good advice to the young people who were taught to respect him and obey his words. Only a man who was known to embody in his own life the excellent principles he uttered was allowed to act as crier. He usually announced that it was time for the young men who were calling upon the young maidens to go home. He spoke impersonally of the conduct of the young people, describing incidents in such a manner that those concerned in them would know to what he referred. He taught sterling principles of character and gave such advice as he thought necessary. Odinigun said that the old man emphasized the teaching that the young people must not steal, also that they must keep away from fire water, use very little tobacco, and never say anything disrespectful concerning women. He told the women that they must keep from quarreling, live peaceably, and not say bad things about each other. The advice to young men and women was, "Obey your parents, take their advice, and respect them. If you live in that way while you are among your own people you will be respected when you go to a strange village."

Mention has been made of the fact that one or more grandparents were usually in every household. A man usually lived with his wife's family, hence the old people were her parents. The grandmother talked tò the mother and told her how to bring up the girls, and the grandfather advised the father how to instruct and bring up the boys. One piece of advice which was strong and often repeated was "if your children go among the neighbors and make a quarrel, don't you take their part. You must bring them home and make them behave them-selves. Do not get into a quarrel with your neighbors because of the quarrels of the children." Another precept was "teach the children what is right to do, and they will live that way and get on well in the world." Nodinens said, "I had four brothers and two sisters. My father gave counsel to the boys and taught them the best way to live, and my mother told the girls how to conduct themselves. The first thing I can remember was my mother's saying, "always be industrious. Get up early and do your work. Do you hear me? Do you hear me? Do you understand?" She took hold of my ear and pulled it hard as she said this, and she kept on until I said that I understood. She told me that I must live a quiet life and be kind to all, especially the old, and listen to the advice of the old. She said that people would respect me if I did this and would be kind to me. She said, "Do not run after a boy. If a young man wants to marry you, let him come here to see you and come here to live with you. This is the reason I am always telling you to be industrious and how to live, so when you have a home of your own you will be industrious and do right to the people around you." She taught me to make mats and bags, to make belts and moccasins, leggings, and coats for my brothers, so they would never lack for these things."

Nodinens added, "I have tried to do as my mother taught me. Now at my age I look back and am so grateful to her for giving me this advice, and I think it is the reason I have been so blessed and prospered all my life." Nodinens said the advice which her father gave to her brothers was similar to that quoted above. He told them not to be idle and "run around" but to hunt and to work so they would be prosperous. She also said that her father told the boys not to destroy birds' nests as "the birds were put here for the good of the earth." Children received their first lessons in the value of plants by being encouraged to gather every flower they saw in the fields. These blossoms were dried, pulverized, and used in the making of a beverage. But at the same time the child learned that some plants had a medicinal value, while all were placed on the earth for the good of mankind.

The companionship of a Chippewa girl and her mother was very close and the child learned many household tasks by watching and helping her mother. Thus, a little girl was early, taught to chop wood and carry it on her back, and as she grew older she carried larger and larger bundles of wood until she could carry enough into the wigwam for the night's use. A girl was taught to make little birch-bark rolls like those which covered the wigwam, her mother saying "you must not grow up to live outdoors and be made fun of because you do not know how to make a good wigwam." She was also taught to make maple sugar, gather wild rice, and do all a woman's tasks. Odinigun said that " a man had no bother thinking he must go home and do this or that, for he knew that his wife would attend to it." He said that if a girl was well brought up and was capable she usually got a good husband. Her reputation often went to other villages, and a young man would seek her out because he had heard that she was quiet and industrious. Such a couple usually had a fine family; the children were well governed and did not quarrel. In concluding this subject Odinigun said that in his old age he noticed that those who had kept the advice of the old people had lived long and led a quiet life, but those who did not regard their advice had had much trouble and died.

A little girl was trained in what might be termed the accomplishments of feminine life, as well as in its household tasks. Her first lessons in applied beadwork were the decoration of her doll's clothing, straight lines, either continuous or interrupted, being the easiest patterns, from which she progressed to diagonal patterns and the familiar "otter-tail pattern." In woven beadwork she frequently began by making a narrow chain with horizontal rows of beads of different colors, two or three rows of each color. This gave pleasure to the eye and involved no counting of the beads except in the multiple of the number of threads on the little loom, less the "end thread." A simple pattern for a child consisted in a stripe of contrasting color down the middle of the chain, after which she might attempt a diagonal or zigzag pattern in two colors. In such easy, yet intelligent, lessons a Chippewa girl was trained by her mother.

PASTIMES FOR LITTLE CHILDREN

The following pastimes show the simple means devised for entertaining little children. A multitude of other pastimes have been forgotten in the advance of the race toward a new mode of life.

1. The summer child: A child born in summer was called a summer child. The first winter in which such a child could talk was usually

when it was about a year and a half old. If the weather were very cold, the child was taught to take a handful of ashes, go to the door of the wigwam and throw the ashes around, saying, "South wind, your child is getting cold." It is said that the weather would then turn warmer. Sometimes, when a shaft of sunlight came through a hole in the wigwam cover, the summer child was told to try to take hold of it, as though it could climb upward on it, and to say, "Summer, summer." It was said that sometimes this action would make the child quite warm.

BABY-SITTING IN CAMP: Big brother is holding his little sibling in a variation of the cradleboard, the so-called "moss bag," which was lined with soft, cleaned moss before the coming of diapers and pampers. The bags, made from buckskin and velvet, are more convenient, at times, to handle and carry around because they lack the heavy wooden frame. The child is first wrapped in a small blanket, then laced firmly inside the bag, arms either folded in or left out. This scene was taken in 1911 among the Wheatgrass Cree near Battleford, Saskatchewan. The boy has on moccasins and a black velvet vest with lots of flowers and designs beaded on it. Behind him are two canvas wall tents, which replaced tipis among some native families soon after the buffalo days ended, around 1880.

2. The winter child: A child born in winter was called a winter child. When he was able to walk around the wigwam he sometimes held up his hands to warm them at the fire. This was said to be an unfailing sign of very cold weather.

3. Stopping a snowstorm: During a heavy snowstorm it is a frequent custom to tell a boy to go out and shoot the snow. The child's father put a piece of birch bark on the end of the child's arrow, fitted it to his bow, and set fire to it, saying, "Shoot ; hit the snow right in the eye." The boy shot the arrow with its flaming tip into the thickly falling snow; then he went into the wigwam and went to bed. It was said that the snow always ceased before he woke in the morning.

4. The new tooth: When one of a child's first teeth came out he was told to take the tooth in one hand and a piece of charcoal in the other hand. Then he was told to throw the tooth toward the east and the charcoal toward the west, saying, "I want a new tooth as soon as possible."

5. Calling the butterflies: By members of the Mississippi and Mille Lac bands of Indians living at White Earth the butterfly was regarded as the "spirit of childish play" and a butterfly was often used as a decoration on children's articles, as well as a figure in birch-bark transparencies. Inquiry among the Red Lake Chippewa did not disclose a similar belief among them. The White Earth Chippewa stated that children were never allowed to destroy butterflies. They were taught to call the butterflies to join in their games, especially in the game of hide and seek. A child would hold its nose between its thumb and forefinger and run about calling "Me-e-mëmgwe" (Butterfly-butterfly). Mrs. Martin said she had often seen the butterflies come when the children called them in this manner. The term for butterfly is "memingwa," but was pronounced as indicated when used in this pastime.

6. The spirit of the woods: "When children went into the woods they were taught to watch and heed the "spirit of the woods." This was said to be like the "spirit of the water" which is mentioned in connection with dreams, and which has power to quiet the waves if so

requested by a person who has dreamed of the water. Children were told that if they were going into danger the spirit of the woods would break a little branch and throw it in front of them as a warning. It is interesting to note the friendly guardianship of the wood spirit; also that waves did not indicate anger on the part of the water spirits.

Among the first playthings given a child was the skin of some small animal filled with maple sugar and imperfectly sewed, so that the child in handling the article and putting it to its mouth would obtain a little of the sugar. Squirrels and other animals were stuffed as playthings for children, wild rice being sometimes used for the purpose.

A Menominee informant said that birds as well as animals were stuffed and used as toys, and that it was customary in old times to tie some small object to a baby's wrist, the object being something that the child could put in its mouth. A peculiar toy described by the Menominee consisted of the leg of a freshly killed deer, a muscle being left so that an older person could pull it, thus causing the toes to move for the amusement of the child. The Menominee also drew pictures on the ground for the entertainment of the children.

Large flat lichens were cut from trees and etched in patterns resembling those on woven-yarn bags. These were used by little girls in their play, being placed along the walls in imitation of the yarn bags in the wigwams. In more recent times bright-colored autumn leaves were used by the children to represent letters, and the children played "post office" receiving these "letters" and pretending to read them. Leaves were selected with distinct markings, which they read as words.

As soon as a boy was able to hold anything in his hands he was given something resembling a bow and arrow, and taught to go through the motions of shooting. A bow and arrows were first given a boy when he was 5 or 6 years of age, and with this he took his first lessons in the craft that was most necessary to a hunter or warrior in the old days. The boy was taught to hold the bow horizontally, the arrow resting on the bow and passing under the bowstring. He held the bow in such a manner that his thumb was inside the bow while the arrow passed between two fingers. The projection at the end of the arrow was held between the thumb and finger of the right hand, making it an easy matter to draw the bow. It was said that boys were encouraged to use this bow and arrows and that they could be trusted not to do any damage with it.

DOLLS

These will be considered in the order of their elaboration. The simplest form of representing a human being was by means of a large tuft of the needles of the Norway pine. This tuft was cut squarely across the end, and about halfway up a part of the needles were cut across, suggesting the length of the arms, or perhaps a shawl hanging from the shoulders. A bit of the wood was left at the top of the tuft suggesting the head. These little figurines were placed upright on a piece of zinc or in a large tin pan which was gently agitated. This motion caused the figurines to tremble in a manner suggesting an Indian dance and even to move back and forth, according to the skill of the person manipulating the tin on which they were placed. Dolls were also made of green basswood leaves and of bright autumn leaves, fastened with little splinters of wood.

Figures of men and women were made from a portion of the root of bulrushes that is below the water. This was partially dried and made into figures by tying it with basswood fibers after which the figures were thoroughly dried and could be handled without breaking.

A step higher in development were the figures of men and women cut from the inner bark of the slippery elm. Attention is directed to the fact that in the types of dolls above mentioned there is no attempt to outline the features of the face. It appears that in this stage of primitive art it was not necessary to show the details of an object; in brief, the article represented nature without being a close imitation of nature. A similar stage of development was noted in the patterns used in beadwork.

Sports and Games for Children

In all outdoor sports the girls were as proficient as the boys. All were expert swimmers. An old woman said, "The children were like ducks, in-and-out of the water all day. They never stopped to take off the little clothing they had on, and their clothes dried on them when they came out of the water."

Marbles : Stones similar to marbles were used by the boys. These stones were of two sorts, spherical and slightly flattened. In playing with these a number of holes about the size of the marbles were made in the ground, the round stones being thrown sideways toward the hole, the object being to place as many stones as possible in the holes.

Deer sticks: A favorite pastime of little boys was to take two sticks and use them in the manner of "arm stilts." By means of these sticks they produced an effect of being four-legged and imitated the motions of a deer, cavorting about and kicking those who happened to be behind them. The sticks are 2 feet 11 inches long, and the bark is removed except for 5 inches at one end.

Spinning stone: This form of top was a favorite plaything of boys and was also used by men. The game implements consisted of a smooth stone of a shape which would spin well and a wooden whip with a leathern thong. The game was usually played on the ice, the stone being set in motion with the fingers and kept in motion by striking it with the whip. The "whip top" is widely used among Indian tribes of the United States and Alaska.

Woman's game: There is a game among the Chippewa which is known as the woman's game, and little girls were early provided with simplified implements of this game, as the boys were provided with simplified bows and arrows. The implements of the woman's game consisted of two long sticks carried by each player and two billets about 3 inches long fastened together by a thong and tossed from one player to another. In the set intended for a little girl there is a notch in one of the sticks, making it easier to catch and hold the thong between the short sticks.

Bunch of grass game: A certain game played by the little girls was a miniature of a woman's game. As played by the little girls the bunch of grass and stick were very small. The manner of play was the same as in the adult game, the grass being tossed upward and caught on the pointed stick.

Playing camp: Boys and girls joined in this sport. They made a little wigwam and "fixed it up," making fire in the center. The boys caught fish, or killed rabbits or birds, and threw them into the wigwam for the girls to cook. The little girls roasted them or cooked them in the ashes, and sometimes were given potatoes to cook in the ashes.

Hide and seek, or the butterfly game: This game was preceded by the drawing of lots. Four sticks were prepared, one of which was longer than the others. A set of these sticks was obtained. The longer was 3 inches in length and the others 2 inches, the four being tied together with basswood fiber. These sticks were held by one of the children, the others being told to draw a stick in turn. The one who drew the longer stick was the one to cover his eyes while the others hid. When all were ready he began his search, singing ("Me-e-mëm-gwe, me-e-mèm-gwe (butterfly, show me where to go)". He held his nose between thumb and fingers as he sang this, giving it a peculiar nasal sound, and he prolonged the first syllable, the rhythm of the call being 1-2-3-4, with the "3-4" corresponding to the two last syllables.

FIVE FINDING A MATE

B oys and girls of the tribal days were often paired up by their parents while still very young. Though this custom may seem rather arbitrary by our modern standards, it generally led to successful marriages, which is more than can often be said today. Of course, back then everyone in the tribe shared the same basic goals and aspirations. Tribal customs dictated the ways of life, which left little for husbands and wives to disagree about, especially in comparison with the lack of standards these days.

Native children had a lot more freedom in their younger years than modern children, but once those times were over, they went right into serious adulthood. In tribal camps there was not really a place for teenage life, as such. Girls in their teen years usually got married, while boys did the hunting and fought with enemies, along with the men. Nowadays, of course, teenagers are as conspicuous a group within Indian tribes as in any other social group.

One old woman we knew got married when she was only seven! Teenage life for her was a time of having children, being a woman, and no parties or boyfriends. We know an old man from the same tribe who got married when he was twelve, though he was the only one in his age group who had a wife. He said his friends teased him about it, especially since the wife was younger and still played with dolls.

Both of these old people had long and prosperous lives with their childhood partners, and both spoke about the need for discipline within the marriage and the family, in terms of fulfilling commitments. In their young days, single parents were almost unknown.

It is a sign of leisure in our own society that we can afford to let our children be teenagers for several years. The reality of daily wilderness life required that everyone in the tribe do whatever work he or she was capable of. Food was of primary concern, and in large families children were often encouraged to marry early, so that they could provide their own. This was especially true if there were several girls in a household. Boys were at least able to hunt, and thus contribute to the larder.

Parents generally had a hand in picking mates for their children, for several reasons. If their child was a girl, they wanted a son-in-law who would treat her kindly; and also one who would treat them well, by supplying them with meat and horses if they should need them. Some well-off parents wanted their children to marry into families like theirs, to ensure continued ambition. Or, rich parents of a girl might select, instead, a very poor boy—even an orphan—who would then be available to take care of their horses, as well as their food needs. Lazy, dirty, or mean children usually ended up being mates to each other, since all the "good ones" would be accounted for. In the case of girls, they might instead become the second or third wife of a successful man, whose family put up with her in return for making her do much of the work. Lazy boys sometimes had to go out and steal a wife from the enemy if no decent girl would have them.

Young girls were often given away for marriage by their parents while quite young, in order to preserve their virginity. Although virginity was often a high tribal virtue, people recognized that girls within such closed societies were under growing pressure to mate with the men around them. Those who were strong enough to resist all temptations were eligible in some tribes for the very highest honor, involving sacred ceremonies for the Sun. Such women have always been few in number, but there are yet a few tribes who have them.

In recent times, there has been a lot of interest shown in "traditional Indian marriages", which are often very colorful and inspiring ceremonies. But very few tribes actually had anything like the marriage ceremonies we envision. Generally, two people became husband and wife after sharing a bed together. The parents might make a big ritual out of exchanging valuable presents, but this had little to do with the couple themselves. They didn't usually stand shyly in the camp circle holding hands, while everyone threw dried berries. Rather, they carried on with their normal daily chores, and that night they slept together. If all was well, they got their own tipi or lodge. Often as not, one moved in with the other, and that one's family!

If there was a ceremony at all, its major significance was the "coming-of-age". From being mere children, the husband and wife suddenly had all the responsibilities of grown-ups. They then went through a period of trial-and-error through which most survived. If the mating didn't work out, the two went back to their respective homes and waited for another try, usually with someone else. In the traditional tribal camps, it was practically a foregone conclusion that males and

Apache mother
and children

females would mate together, and the emphasis was on becoming mates for life.

It should be pointed out that many young people did marry the mates of their choice, even if not always with the support of their parents. Boys, especially, were often allowed to select a potential wife, whose parents were then approached by a relative or friend bearing gifts with the request. If the girl's parents were kind people, they would ask her opinion on the matter; if not, they would accept or reject the boy based on their own judgment. There were no firm rules about this, each family deciding how to handle the marriage in their own way; except, again, that tribal custom decreed that two mates sleeping together were automatically husband and wife.

Omaha Marriage Customs

(Alice C. Fletcher and Francis La Flesche, *The Omaha Tribe*)

When a young man asked the hand of a girl in marriage, he observed a certain conventional form of address. The words were not always the same, but the aspect put on the proposal was practically uniform. The young man extolled the girl and her relations, and did not vaunt himself. He pleaded his constancy and asked, rather than demanded, that she become his wife, craving it as a boon. There were signals, other than songs or cute calls, to let a girl know her lover was near. A tent pole might fall or some other noise made which she would know how to interpret, and so be able to meet the young man if a meeting had been agreed on.

Marriage was usually by elopement. The claims on a girl (by those) holding a potential right to marry her almost necessitated her escaping secretly, if she would exercise her free choice in the matter of a husband. During their courtship, when a young couple determined on taking the final step of marriage, they agreed to meet some evening. The youth generally rode to a place near the lodge of the girl and gave the proper signal; she stepped out and they galloped off to one of his relations. In a day or two, the young man took the girl to his father's lodge where, if she was received as his wife, all claims by other men as to marriage were cancelled by this act. Gifts had to be made to the girl's parents and shared with her relatives, in order to ratify the marriage.

To bring this about, the father of the young man made a feast and invited the relatives of the girl. When this invitation was accepted and the presents received, the marriage was considered settled beyond all dispute. In the course of a few months, the father of the bride generally presented his daughter with return gifts about equal in value to those he had received, and the young husband was expected to work for his father-in-law for a year or two. This latter claim was frequently exacted rigidly, and the father-in-law was sometimes a tyrant over his son-in-law's affairs.

A state of social equality existed between men and women. Tribal custom favored chastity, and those who practiced it stood higher in public esteem than those who did not. If a woman had committed indiscretions in her youth, yet later led a moral life, her former acts were remembered, but weren't held against her, or her husband and children. Both men and women were allowed to win back their past position by subsequent good conduct.

Cohabitation constituted marriage, whether the relationship was of long or short duration, provided that the woman was not the wife of another man—in which case the relationship was a social and punishable offense. Prostitution, as practiced in a white community, did not exist in the tribe.

The father was recognized as having the highest authority over all members of the family, although in most matters pertaining to the welfare of the children, the mother exercised almost equal authority. During the lifetime of the parents, the uncle was as alert as their father to defend the children or to avenge a wrong done them. The children always regarded their uncle as their friend, ever ready to help them.

When a marriage was arranged by a girl's parents, with or without her consent, it was apt to be with a man in mature life and established position. The would-be husband made large presents to the girl's parents and relatives. When the time came for the marriage, the girl was well-dressed and mounted on a pony. Accompanied by four old men, she was then taken to the lodge of her husband. Young men derided this kind of marriage by saying, "An old man cannot win a girl; he can win only her parents."

A man rarely had more than two wives, and these were generally sisters or aunt and niece. These complex families were usually harmonious, and sometimes there seemed to be little difference in the feeling of the children toward the two women who were wives to their father.

If a man abused his wife, she left him; and her conduct was justified by her relations and by tribal opinion. As the tent or dwelling always belonged to the woman, the unkind husband found himself homeless. The young children generally remained with the mother, although the father's brothers would be expected to assist the woman in their support. Generally speaking, the family was fairly stable; tribal sentiment did not favor the changing of the marriage relation from mere caprice.

Winnebago Marriage Customs

(Paul Radin, *The Winnebago Tribe*)

Young girls and women are also encouraged to fast to obtain the war honors. Fasting at puberty by girls was inseparably connected with their retirement to menstrual lodges. Sometimes there was only one girl in each menstrual lodge, and sometimes there were as many as three. When a woman was finished in the menstrual lodge, she bathed herself and put on an entirely new suit of clothes. Then her home was purified with red-cedar leaves and all the sacred bundles and medicines removed. Only then could she enter her parents' lodge. As soon as she returned to her parents' lodge after her first menstrual flow, she was regarded as ready to be wooed and married.

Girls were usually married as soon as they reached marriageable age, and the same was probably true of men. In most cases, marriage was arranged by the parents, and it rarely happened that the young people refused to abide by the decision—a fact that seems to have been due, not so much to implicit obedience, as to the wise precautions taken by the parents in mating their children. . . . In former times, children were betrothed to each other at an early age. At the betrothal, presents were exchanged between the parents. . . .

Generally, a man took but one wife, although he was permitted to marry more than one if he wished. In polygamous marriages the second wife was usually a niece or a sister of the first wife. It was the wife who often induced her husband to marry her own niece. This she did if she noticed that he was getting tired of her or losing his interest in her.

There was no ceremony connected with marriage. As soon as the customary presents were exchanged, the man came to the woman's lodge and the marriage was consummated.

A man generally lived with his parents-in-law during the first two years after his marriage. During these two years, he was practically the servant of his father-in-law, hunting, fishing, and performing minor services for him. After the first two years, he returned to his father's lodge, where his seat had always been kept for him. With his own folks, he stayed as long as he wished, leaving it generally as soon as he had one child.

In olden times, when it was customary for those Winnebago who lived in permanent villages to occupy the long, gable-roofed lodges large enough to house as many as 40 people, the man and his family generally alternated between parents.

Sioux Maiden's Feast

(Charles Alexander Eastman, *Indian Boyhood*)

One bright summer morning, while we were still at our meal of jerked buffalo meat, we heard the herald of the Wahpeton band upon his calico pony as he rode around our circle: "White Eagle's daughter, the maiden Red Star, invites all the maidens . . . to come and partake of her feast. It will be in the Wahpeton camp, before the sun reaches the middle of the sky. All pure maidens are invited. Red Star also invites the young men to be present, to see that no unworthy maiden should join in the feast."

The herald soon completed the rounds of the different camps, and it was not long before the girls began to gather in great numbers.

This particular feast was looked upon as a semi-sacred affair. It would be desecration for any to attend who was not perfectly virtuous. Hence, it was regarded as an opportune time for the young men to satisfy themselves as to who were the virtuous maids of the tribe.

There were apt to be surprises before the end of the day. Any young man was permitted to challenge any maiden whom he knew to be unworthy. But woe to the one who could not prove his case. It meant little short of death to the man who endeavored to disgrace a woman without cause.

The youths had a similar feast of their own, in which the eligibles were those who had never spoken to a girl in the way of courtship. It was considered ridiculous to do so before attaining some honor as a warrior, and the novices prided themselves greatly upon their self-control.

From the various camps the girls came singly or in groups, dressed in bright-colored calicoes or in heavily fringed and beaded buck-skin. Their smooth cheeks and the central part of their glossy hair was touched with vermillion. All brought with them wooden basins to eat from.

The maidens' circle was formed about a cone-shaped rock that stood upon its base. This was painted red. Beside it two new arrows were lightly stuck into the ground. This is a sort of altar, to which each maiden comes before taking her assigned place in the circle, and lightly touches, first the stone, and then the arrows. By this oath, she declares her purity.

Whenever a girl approaches the altar there is a stir among the spectators, and sometimes a rude youth would call out: "Take care! You will overturn the rock, or pull out the arrows!" Such a remark makes the girls nervous, and especially one who is not sure of her composure.

Immediately behind the maidens' circle is the old women's, or chaperons', circle. This second circle is almost as interesting to look at as the inner one. The old women watched every movement of their respective charges with the utmost concern, having previously instructed them how they should conduct themselves in any event.

The whole population of the region had assembled, and the maidens came shyly into the circle. The simple ceremonies observed prior to the serving of the food were in progress, when among a group of Wahpeton Sioux young men there was a stir of excitement. All the maidens glanced nervously toward the scene of the disturbance. Soon a tall youth emerged from the throng of spectators and advanced toward the circle. Every one of the chaperons glared at him as if to deter him from his purpose. But with a steady step he passed them by and approached the maidens' circle.

At last, he stopped behind a pretty Assiniboine maiden of good family and said:

"I am sorry, but, according to custom, you should not be here. "

The girl arose in confusion, but she soon recovered her self-control. "What do you mean?" she demanded, indignantly. "Three times you have come to court me, but each time I have refused to listen to you. I turned my back upon you. Twice I was with Mashtinna. She can tell the people that this is true. The third time, I had gone for water when you intercepted me and begged me to stop and listen. I refused, because I did not know you. My chaperon, Makatopawee, knows that I was gone but a few minutes. I never saw you anywhere else."

The young man was unable to answer this unmistakable statement of facts, and it became apparent that he had sought to revenge himself for her repulse.

"Woo! woo! Carry him out!" was the order of the chief of the Indian police, and the audacious youth was hurried away into the nearest ravine to be chastised.

The young woman who had thus established her good name returned to the circle, and the feast was served. The "maidens' song" was sung, and four times they danced in a ring around the altar. Each maid, as she departed, once more took her oath to remain pure until she should meet her husband.

Hidatsa Courting Customs

(Excerpt by Buffalo-bird Woman from Gilbert L. Wilson, *Agriculture of the Hidatsa Indians: An Indian Interpretation*)

The youths of the village used to go about all the time seeking the girls; this indeed was almost all they did. Of course, when the girls were on the (garden) watcher's stage, the boys were pretty sure to come around. Sometimes two youths came together, sometimes but one. If there were relatives at the watcher's stage the boys would stop and drink or eat; they did not try to talk to the girls, but would come around smiling and try to get the girls to smile back.

A girl that was not a youth's sweetheart never talked to him. This rule was observed at all times. Even when a boy was a girl's sweetheart, or "love-boy", as we called him, if there were other persons around, she did not talk to him unless these happened to be relatives. Boys who came out to the watchers' stage, getting no encouragement from the girls there, soon went away.

A very young girl was not permitted to go to the watcher's stage unless an old woman went along to take care of her. In olden days, mothers watched their daughters very carefully.

Most of the songs that were sung on the watchers' stage were love songs, but not all. One that little girls were fond of singing—girls that is of about twelve years of age—was as follows:

You bad boys, you are all alike!
Your bow is like a bent basket hoop;
You poor boys, you have to run on the prairie barefoot;
Your arrows are fit for nothing but to shoot up into the sky!

Here is another song, sung by a girl to another whom she loves as her own sister. We call her "ikupa," which has about the same meaning as your word, "chum".

"My ikupa, what do you wish to see?" you said to me.
What I wish to see is the corn silk coming out on the growing ears;
But what you wish to see is that naughty young man coming!

Here is a song that we sang to tease young men that were going by:

You young men of the Dog society, you said to me, "When I go to the
east on a war party, you will hear news of me, how brave I am"
I have heard news of you;
When the fight was on, you ran and hid! And you think you are a
brave young man! Behold, you have joined the Dog society.
Therefore, I call you just plain dog!

READY FOR THE DANCE: "Cool" for this Nez Perce teenager in 1910 meant a decorated otter fur hat over his long, loose hair, an otter-skin sash across his chest decorated with round mirrors, and a long white weasel skin—all of it for good luck. Also in style was the long striped shirt, woolen breech-cloth and leggings, fully-beaded moccasins, and trade blanket thrown over one arm (in case it gets cold or some equally 'cool' cutie in a long dress comes along.)

Courting at the Corn Harvest

(Excerpt by Buffalo-bird Woman from Gilbert L. Wilson, *Agriculture of the Hidatsa Indians: An Indian Interpretation*)

Having arrived at the field, and started a fire or the feast, all of our family who had come out to work sat down and began to husk the corn. Word had been sent beforehand that we were going to give a husking feast, and the invited helpers soon appeared. There was no particular time set for their coming, but we expected them in one of the morning hours.

For the most part, these were young men from nineteen to thirty years of age, but a few old men would probably be in the company; and these were welcomed and given a share of the feast.

There might be twenty-five or thirty of the young men. They were paid for their labor with the most given them to eat; and each carried a sharp stick on which he skewered the meat he could not eat, to take home.

The husking season was looked upon as a time of jollity, and youths and maidens dressed and decked themselves for the occasion. Of course, each young man gave particular help to the garden of his sweetheart. Some girls were more popular than others.

The young men were apt to vie with one another at the husking pile of an attractive girl.

Some of the young men rode ponies, and when her corn pile had been husked, a youth would sometimes lend his pony to his sweetheart for her to carry home her corn. She loaded the pony with loose ears in bags, bound on either side of the saddle, or with strings of braided corn laid upon the pony's back.

Courting in Sioux Tipi Camps

(Charles Alexander Eastman, *Indian Boyhood*)

Indian courtship is very peculiar in many respects; but when you study their daily life you will see the philosophy of their etiquette of love-making. There was no parlor courtship; the life was largely out-of-doors, which was very favorable to the young men.

In nomadic life, where the female members of the family have entire control of domestic affairs, the work is divided among them all. Very often, the bringing of the wood and water devolves upon the young maids, and the spring or the woods become the battle-ground of love's warfare. The nearest water may be some distance from the camp, which is all the better. Sometimes, if there is no wood to be had, one would see the young women scattered all over the prairie, gathering buffalo chips for fuel.

This is the way the red men go about to induce the aboriginal maids to listen to their suit. As soon as the youth has returned from the warpath or the chase, he puts on his porcupine quill-embroidered moccasins and leggings, and folds his best robe about him. He brushes his long, glossy hair with a brush made from the tail of the porcupine, perfumes it with scented grass or leaves, then arranges it in two plaits with an otter skin or some other ornament. If he is a warrior, he adds an eagle feather or two.

If he chooses to ride, he takes his best pony. He jumps upon its bare back, simply throwing a part of his robe under him to serve as a saddle, and holding the end of a lariat tied about the animal's neck. He guides him altogether by the motions of his body. These wily ponies seem to enter into the spirit of the occasion, and very often capture the eyes of the maid by their graceful movements, in perfect obedience to their master.

The general custom is for the young men to pull their robes over their heads, leaving only a slit to look through. Sometimes the same is done by the maiden, especially in public courtship.

He approaches the girl while she is coming from the spring. He takes up his position directly in her path. If she is in a hurry, or does not care to stop, she goes around him; but if she is willing to stop and listen, she puts down on the ground the vessel of water she is carrying.

Very often, at the first meeting, the maiden does not know who her lover is. He does not introduce himself immediately, but waits until a second meeting. Sometimes, she does not see his face at all; and then she will try to find out who he is and what he looks like, before they meet again. If he is not a desirable suitor, she will go with her chaperon and end the affair there.

There are times when maidens go in twos, and then there must be two young men to meet them.

There is courtship in the night time; either in the early part of the evening, on the outskirts of dances and other public affairs, or after everybody is supposed to be asleep. This is the secret courtship. The youth may pull up the tent pins just back of his sweetheart and speak with her during the night. He must be a smart young man to do that undetected, for the grandmother, her chaperon, is usually "all ears".

Elopements are common. There are many reasons for a girl or a youth to defer their wedding. It may be from personal pride of one or both. The well-born are married publicly, and many things are given away in their honor. The maiden may desire to attend a certain number of maidens' feasts before marrying. The youth may be poor, or he may wish to achieve another honor before surrendering to a woman.

Sometimes, a youth is so infatuated with a maiden that he will follow her to any part of the country, even after their respective bands have separated for the season. I know of one such case. Patah Tankah had courted a distant relative of my uncle for a long time. There seemed to be some objection to him on the part of the girl's parents, although the girl herself was willing.

The large camp had been broken up for the fall hunt, and my uncle's band went one way, the young man's family went in the other direction. After three days' traveling, we came to a good hunting-ground, and made camp. One evening somebody saw the young man. He had been following his sweetheart and sleeping out-of-doors all that time, although the nights were already frosty and cold. He met her every day in secret and she brought him food, but he would not come near the teepee. Finally her people yielded, and she went back with him to his band.

When we lived our natural life, there was much singing of war songs, medicine, hunting, and love songs. Sometimes there were few words or none, but everything was understood by the inflection. From this, I have often thought that there must be a language of dumb beasts. The crude musical instrument of the Sioux—the flute—was made to appeal to the susceptible ears of the maidens late into the night. There comes to me now the picture of two young men with their robes over their heads, and only a portion of the hand-made and carved "chotanka" (the flute) protruding from its folds. I can see all the maidens slyly turning their heads to listen. Now I hear one of the youths begin to sing a plaintive serenade as in days gone by:

> *"Listen! You will hear of him---*
> *Hear of him who loves you!*
> *Maiden, you will hear of him---*
> *Hear of him who loves you, who loves you!*
> *Listen! he will shortly go*
> *Seeking your ancestral foe!*

Wasula feels that she must come out, but she has no good excuse, so she stirs up the embers of the fire and causes an unnecessary smoke in the teepee. Then she has an excuse to come out and fix up the tent caps. She takes a long time to adjust these pointed ears of the teepee, with their long poles, for the wind seems to be unsettled.

Finally, "chotanka" ceases to be heard. In a moment, a young man appears, ghost-like, at the maiden's side.

"So it is you, is it?" she asks.

"Is your grandmother in?" he inquires.

"What a brave man you are, to fear an old woman! We are free; the country is wide. We can go away, and come back when the storm is over."

"Ho," he replies. "It is not that I fear her, or the consequences of an elopement. I fear nothing except that we may be separated!"

The girl goes into the lodge for a moment, and then slips out once more. "Now," she exclaims, "to the wood or the prairie! I am yours!" They disappear into the darkness.

Blackfoot Tipi-Creeping on the Canadian Prairies

(Told by Ben Calf Robe at the HungryWolf kitchen table in 1977)

When I was young, parents were still very strict with their children—especially the girls. When boys start to have girlfriends, they have to figure out all kinds of ways to sneak around and meet with each other. The ones who were pretty brave used to go right into the tipis where their girls lived, way late, after everybody was asleep. Sometimes some pretty funny things happened that way.

One time I was going around with my best friend, singing around the Sun Dance camp late at night, as was our custom. We stopped by this white tent that belonged to a Blood family. Inside there was a real pretty girl—we were all after her, she was so nice. My friend and I crawled under a wagon by this tent to take a rest. Pretty soon, two other fellows came along—they were older than us. They didn't see us resting in the dark. The one fellow told the other, "I'll go in first, and you watch for me. Scratch on the tent if anybody comes along."

This was a new white tent that the girl was living in. It had a picket rope that went down the front. They pulled the picket pin up so the rope would be out of the way. But the one who was staying out tied the end of that rope to his friend's overalls. The one going in didn't know it. He went on in and there was a tin stove in the way. It was dark, and he must have tripped over something. Pretty soon we heard the stove rattle and a dog jumped up and started barking. The fellow just threw himself out the door and started running. Then the rope gave out and it looked just like somebody threw him back into the tent. He jumped back up and started running again, and the same thing happened. By this time the dog was really barking and everybody in the tent was awake. My friend and I were laughing like crazy. Finally, he noticed that the rope was tied to his overalls, and he tore it off and ran away. All the dogs were barking in the camp, and the neighbors were calling out to see what was going on.

Another time, two friends went to a tipi where their girlfriend lived. One stayed outside and watched, while the other one snuck in. He knew where the girl was sleeping, but he didn't know that she had a small hawk for a pet. Sometimes, in the past, the people used to keep wild birds and animals for pets. The hawk was perched on one of the backrests by the girl's bed. When the boy got close, the bird made a sound, like "Hagh, hagh." The boy thought it was his sweetheart calling to him, and he went closer. "Hagh, hagh," the bird said. The boy whispered, "What are you saying?" The bird just kept going, "Hagh, hagh." Finally, the boy put his hand on the backrest to lean down, and the bird scratched him and bit him on the hand. The boy jumped up and got scared, and the then bird screamed aloud and flapped his wings, and everybody in the tipi woke up. The boy ran out real quick!"

Plains Cree Customs

(David G. Mandelbaum, *The Plains Cree*)

While parents customarily selected their child's spouse, courtship and love affairs leading to marriage were not unknown. A man would lie in wait for a girl whom he liked while she was berrying or on her way to fetch wood or water. He would try to engage her in conversation; if she were willing to talk with him, he knew that his suit was well received. After several such conversations, either the boy or the girl, or both, might ask their parents to make the marriage arrangements.

Quite different from this pre-nuptial courtship were the love-making escapades of young men. An unmarried young man would forewarn a girl that he intended to visit her at night and would steal up to her tipi. Having previously ascertained on which side of the tipi the girl slept, he would reach under the cover and gently wake her. When she felt her lover's hand she took his fingers and played with them. This finger play was the prelude to more intimate caresses. If her parents became aware of his presence, they would drive him off. No other punishment was inflicted.

DESERT BABY: Styles and customs varied, but every tribe had its own kind of safety wrapping for caring and transporting babies, and these styles are still continued today. This is the simple version of a Navajo cradleboard, its frame made from strips of cottonwood and willow, with a blanket and some muslin used for the wrapping and head cover, and laced up firmly with a long buckskin thong. Both containers provide not only safety and protection, but they also get small children used to being still for long periods at a time-something vital in a life full of wild animal hunting and being on guard from enemy attacks, although these were no longer factors in the life of this 1940's baby.

Unmarried young women were always chaperoned and escorted when they went out of camp. If a young man came upon a girl alone, she was fair game for him. Apparently, women rarely repulsed such advances and never made an outcry. To discourage these attempts women sometimes tied thongs around their thighs and over the pubic region.

Virginity was not of such great concern among the Plains Cree as it was among some of the neighboring tribes. A bride who was also a virgin was prized, but if she were not, it made no great difference. An unmarried girl who gave birth to a child was married off to an elderly or poor husband if the father of the child were unwilling to marry her. If she thereafter comported herself with modesty and dignity, no stigma was attached to her or to the child.

Chippewa Puberty Customs

(Frances Densmore, *Chippewa Customs*)

At the time of her maturity a young girl was required to isolate herself for four days and nights. Her mother made a little wigwam for her at some distance from the lodge, and it is said that in old days she was allowed absolutely no food during this period. A feast was given after her maturing, and she continued her fast until that time. In later days an older sister or other relative brought a little food to the girl. During her isolation she was not allowed to scratch her hair or body with her hands, a stick being provided for that purpose.

The writer's informant said that during the first summer of her womanhood she was not allowed to taste any fruit, berries, or vegetables until the proper ceremony had been enacted. The first fruit was the strawberry, which she gathered. Her parents invited the Mide and others to the feast. Each had a dish of berries, and she had one for herself. The old Mide drummed and sang, then he held a spoonful of the berries to her lips, but as she was about to take it he withdrew it. This was repeated four times, and the fifth time he gave her the berries.

Then she took her dish of berries and ate with the others. This was a great trial to the child who hungered for the fresh fruit, but in it we see the teaching of patience and the discipline which underlies so many Indian customs. The same procedure was repeated with the first of every product of nature, even to the wild rice of the autumn.

At about the same age a boy was required to undergo a fast in which he hoped and expected to obtain a dream or vision. The father taught the boy to prepare for this and insisted that he persevere until he secured the dream. The boy blackened his face with charcoal and usually went away from home for his fast. Sometimes the father took the boy a considerable distance and made a nest for him in a tree. He left the boy there several days, going occasionally to see if he was all right. It was not unusual for a boy to make several attempts before he secured a dream, but complete failures were very rare. Odinigun said that he prepared himself by fasting. In his first attempt to secure a dream he scarcely tasted food or water for eight days, but he saw no vision. The next time he fasted for 10 days. He said that "by that time his mind was clear" and he knew that he would have power to heal the sick. It was not stated that he received a song in this dream, though he may have done so. A song that he used in healing the sick is recorded; the words are, "In a dream I was instructed to do this." The melody is one of unusual vigor and force.

A feast was held when a boy killed his first game. Henry Selkirk said that the first game he killed was a wild canary. He hung it up to wait until he had enough food to give a feast in honor of the event but it was so long before he had enough that the little bird dried up. In older times, when the tribal customs were strictly observed, he would have provided a simple repast, perhaps rice and dried blueberries, or corn, fish, or potatoes, and would have asked five or six old men to the feast. They would have "talked to the manido and made petitions concerning the boy and his family."

COURTSHIP AND MARRIAGE

Young maidens of the Chippewa were closely guarded and were modest in their behavior toward the young men of the tribe. If a young man wished to call upon a young woman he talked first with the older people who lived next to the door of the lodge. He might then proceed to the middle of the lodge, where the young people lived, and talk with the girl in a low tone, but she was not allowed to leave the lodge with him. If a young man came to call rather late in the evening when the fire had burned low the mother or grandmother would rise and stir up the fire so that it burned brightly, then light her pipe and sit up and smoke. The young man could continue his call, but was conscious of being watched. The young men played the "courting flute" in the evenings, but it was never permitted that a young girl leave the lodge in response to the flute.

If a young man's intentions were serious, he killed a deer or some other animal and brought it to the girl's parents. This was to indicate his ability and intention to provide well for his family. If the parents approved of the young man, they asked him to stay and share the feast. This was understood as an acceptance of his wish to marry their daughter, and he was allowed to come and go with more freedom than formerly.

Jealousy among the young girls was a marked feature of Chippewa life and frequently resulted in spirited fighting. The hair seems to have been the special point of attack, being ferociously pulled and frequently the braid being cut of with a knife. The clothing was torn, but slapping with the hand was not a method of this conflict. It was said that a girl who "flirted with several young men" was punished by them, an instance of this sort happening at White Earth in recent rears. One of the young men took the girl into the country, leaving her to find her way home alone. She was waylaid by others of the group, her clothing was torn, and she was thrown into a mudhole.

The young couple might go away quietly for a few days, or they might go at once to live in a lodge of their own. The first-named custom was usually followed if the couple intended to live with the woman's parents. It was the usual custom for a girl to remain at home for a while after her marriage, after which time the couple might, if they desired build a lodge of their own or, occasionally they might live with the husband's parents. Mrs. Julia Spears, who was 88 years old when giving the information, said she remembered an instance which occurred in 1848 among the Bad River band of Chippewa, near the present site of Odanah, Wisconsin. The chief had a daughter of whom he was very fond. His wife built a wigwam for the young couple near their own, furnishing it with new floor mats and other articles. When the young people were ready to begin life together they quietly took up their abode in the wigwam which had been provided for them.

In early days, if a couple living in a lodge of their own could not get along together, the wife went back to her own people and the man could do as he liked. It was said that "if she got over her pouting spell she might go back to him." A man might have two or three wives and all lived in the same lodge, each having her appointed part of the lodge. The writer witnessed a ceremony in the house of a Chippewa at Grand Portage who had two wives. Two of his sons lived with them and the family seemed to be living harmoniously. A Canadian Chippewa said that many Indians had two wives, adding that "the man sat between them." He said that in old times some men had five wives, and that one was the "head wife" and the only one who had children.

On being questioned concerning the courting customs among the Canadian Chippewa he said that he never heard of a courting song except that sung at a dance where all could hear it. He said that for such an occasion a man might "make up a song on account of some girl." This statement was translated back into Chippewa for him in order that there might be no misunderstanding of his meaning. He said that his people had a "long whistle" which the young men played so the girls might hear.

PRECARIOUS BALANCE: This studio photo of a Nez Perce baby in its cradleboard was taken about 1910, but it reminds me of a frightening event that took place about sixty-some years later, when my son, Okan, was a baby. We were eating a a restaurant and had him in a cradleboard similar to this one, leaning against a chair, as here, except that the bottom of his board was, luckily, on the floor. Without a warning, the whole thing suddenly fell slowly forward, the soft sunshade doing little keep Okan's face from bouncing directly off the hardwood floor. Tough little guy that he was, he suffered nothing more that a shock to his dignity, which resulted in no more than a few moments of crying. The child in this photograph would definitely have a longer plunge. The top of his cradleboard is fully-beaded, while the lower bag is made of soft deerskin, laced neatly shut and decorated with strings of glass and shell beads, coins, and two large pink conch shells.

SIX

SOME CHILDHOOD STORIES

A Typical Summer Day for a Hidatsa Boy

(Told by Wolf Chief August 1913, except from Gilbert L. Wilson, *The Horse and the Dog in Hidatsa Culture*)

I will now describe a typical day's herding by boys. Let us suppose that I was about fourteen or fifteen years of age, and that the time of year was about the present date. I recollect very well what occurred one particular day about this time of the year, and will tell about it.

I arose after the sun was up, probably about eight or nine o'clock. Often, though not always, I went for a morning bath in the Missouri. In that case, I proceeded to the river in moccasins, breechcloth, and robe. While I bathed, I drank great quantities of the river water. When I was through bathing, I drew on my robe. Sometimes I rubbed my body with white clay. This made my body feel light. I let my hair hang loose, as it was wet from the bath in the river.

I returned home and put on my leggings and my shirt of white sheeting. Although I did not always wear my leggings during the night, I had slept in both leggings and shirt the previous night, but had taken them off to go to the bath. If I slept without my leggings, I always laid them beside my bed in readiness for the morning.

The rest of the family had eaten their morning meal while I was at the river. My mother gave me my breakfast when I came in. In a wooden bowl she had put boiled dried meat and a mess of parched cornmeal boiled with dried squash. She had parched the corn in a frying pan until brown, stirring it with a stick to keep from burning. She pounded the parched grain to meal in a wooden mortar. When she had brought the squash to a boil, she added the meal. To eat the mess, I probably had a buffalo horn spoon. Sometimes I ate with a mussel shell, or even with one of the big spoons made of a Rocky Mountain sheep horn. The broth in which the dried meat had been boiled was served in a tin cup for a hot drink, as we now serve coffee.

Breakfast eaten, my father said to me, "It is time for you to take out the horses. Keep careful watch in the hills. If you see any strangers who look like enemies, hasten back to the village. Leave your lariat on the neck of your saddle horse and let it drag, so that if an enemy appears, you can quickly catch your horse."

My mother handed me my midday lunch, a double handful of whole parched corn, mixed with minced pieces of dried kidney fats. It was tied up in a heart skin, which I fastened by a string to my belt over my left hip. I also picked out four long ears of white corn from the harvest of the previous year and tied them up in a piece of cloth. Around this bundle I passed a piece of thong, tied the ends in a loop, passed my left arm through the loop, and so carried the bundle slung on my left elbow.

I caught one of the mares in the corral, and put on her a halter made of a flat rawhide lariat. "That is right," said my father, "drive the horses to the river and let them swim to cool off their bodies, that they may better enjoy their grazing."

As I started off on my mare, my father said, "If you meet enemies while you are guarding your horses, try to escape and return home. If you cannot escape, stand against them like a man and make good your arrows!"

I had an unbacked self bow of chokecherry wood, and a quiver of arrows that I carried on my back. The bow case and quiver were of one piece. Of the three kinds of arrows in my quiver, five or six had iron heads and were feathered with prairie-chicken feathers; two were blunt-headed; and seven or eight were pointed wooden shafts. The last two kinds were feathered with duck or owl feathers.

The blunt-headed arrows were for birds, those with iron heads for enemies, and those of pointed wood for gophers and small game. With these last, we also played arrow games.

My father was an arrow-maker, and had made all my arrows for me. They were therefore, quite handsome. They were feathered with plumes from the wing of an owl, a prairie chicken, or a duck.

I wore my hair loose. I did not wear a braided scalplock. When an enemy fell, the first man to strike coup on his body cut out the crown; and the others who also struck coup would, in a twinkling, strip the whole skull of the scalp. We banged the front of our hair and combed it back. The hair was cut short below each ear. That on the back of the head was let grow, and sometimes tied in a bunch, or knot, much as white women do.

In olden times, Hidsatsa women did not braid their hair as they do now, but made a knot of it over the forehead.

Well, as I have said, I drove the herd down to the river, at a place west of the village. After the horses had drunk their fill, I forced them into the water and made them swim or wade to their full depth. Then I dismounted, let my mare drink, and drove her into the water. Holding her by the lariat, I made her wade almost beyond her depth.

After watering the horses at the river, I drove them about a mile from the village, where I found some of my boy friends, who had reached the grazing grounds before me. They were Iduhic, or "Stands-up"—seventeen years old; and Idocic, or "Garter-snake"—sixteen years old. As nearly as I can recollect, I was nearly, or quite, fifteen years old at the time. My two friends were hunting buffalo birds, or cowbirds, among the horses. These birds are dark brown, or black.

After driving my horses into the grazing herd, I dismounted and hobbled my mare, leaving the long lariat on her neck with the end trailing on the ground. I found the two boys had already killed three birds, which they had laid beside their two little bundles of parched corn, brought for their lunch. "Have you shot some birds already?" I asked. "Yes," they answered, "but they are getting scarce now, for we have frightened them. We find it hard to get near any now."

As I talked to the boys, I looked about me. In all directions, within a radius of a quarter- or half-mile, were scattered herds of horses, grazing. Boys were herding most of them, but in the distance I saw one man guarding a herd. I added my horses to those of my two friends. One of these had five horses, while the other had about ten; so there must have been about twenty-seven horses in the herd we were guarding.

We now started to hunt gophers. With some hair that I pulled from the mane of my mare, I made a snare and tied it to the end of my lariat. I set the noose in a gopher's hole. Soon the gopher thrust out his head and I drew the noose taut. The little animal tried to get back into his hole, but I hurried up to it, while holding onto the lariat and passing it through my hands, hand-over-hand. When I reached the hole I drew the gopher out and with a quick swing of the noose, dashed it against the ground, killing it. This had to be done quickly, for a gopher can bite. In this manner, we caught about eight gophers, which we took to the place where we had left our lunch.

"It is now noon." said Stands-up. "I will go to the village and bring some fire." He ran off afoot. Meanwhile, we other two boys went down into the timber a quarter-mile away, and brought dry wood for fuel.

We were first to return, but Stands-up soon joined us, bringing some coals of fire in a pail. We built a fire by placing the coals on the ground and laying little sticks on them, blowing the coals with our mouths. We added larger sticks and soon had a good fire. First, we roasted the birds. A sharpened stick was thrust into the mesh at the vent and I held the bird over the fire with this stick until it was roasted. The entrails were not drawn, neither were the feathers plucked.

When roasted, I broke the bird open and threw the entrails away. I plucked out the wing feathers and stumps of the smaller feathers with my fingers and threw them away, also. I ate the bird, biting the flesh off with my teeth; I did not pull it of with my fingers. We ate none of the corn with the roasted birds at this time. Of course, each of the other boys, as well as myself, roasted and ate a bird.

Then we roasted gophers. First, we opened the gophers and drew out the entrails with our fingers. The lips of the opening made in the carcass of the gopher for the purpose of removing the entrails, were now skewered together by a spit thrust in near the tail. The carcass was held in the fire until the hair was singed, when it was taken out and scraped with a stick to remove the charred hair. It was then held about five inches from the fire, being turned, now with one side, now with the other, toward the fire. The spit was held in the hand.

Each boy roasted the gopher he ate. In all, we ate five gophers, dividing them between us equally. We left three gophers unroasted, but before the fire died down, we singed the hair of these three and put the carcasses away with the corn we had brought for lunch, covering both gophers and corn with a blanket.

We buried the fire, digging a shallow hole and raking the coals into it. We covered the coals with dried horse dung, and put earth over this. We knew the fire would smolder beneath, until we wanted it again.

We noticed now, that some of the herders were driving their horses to water, so we knew it was time for us to do likewise. I caught and unhobbled my grey mare; for, when I began to snare gophers, I had taken the lariat off her neck.

There was a pond not far away, but the water was not good to drink, as there were little worms in it. We watered our horses at the Missouri, and we ourselves drank freely and also bathed. Meanwhile, we had tied our riding horses each to a good big stone, usually about a foot thick, giving the lariat a turn or two about the stone.

After our bath, we got our riding horses and went up the bank to find the rest of the herd already halfway back to the grazing grounds. They were going along at a leisurely pace, stopping now and then to graze. We caught up to them and drove them to our camp again. Here, I hobbled my mare, letting the lariat drag.

We now ate our parched corn. We opened the fire and found the coals still glowing. We added fuel and roasted the three gophers we had saved, each boy eating one. The gophers were fat and made us feel good. I also parched two of the ears of corn I had brought. I made a little bed of coals, laid the ears of corn upon it, and rolled them about with a stick, until they were parched brown. I liked corn parched in this way. The two ears I had not used, I kept to take back home with me. "These are fine ears," I thought. "I chose them because they were the most select, and I may want them again."

After our meal we began again to catch gophers; but as we had been hunting them all morning, they had become frightened and were slow to show themselves. "I know how to catch these gophers," said Garter-snake, at last. "Once before when I was hunting them, they became frightened and did not show themselves, so we poured water down their holes. This made them come up."

"You go to the village and bring us a pail," said Stands-up and Garter-snake to me. I ran off to the village and soon returned with the pail. We also had the small one in which we had brought the fire. We filled the two pails at the pond and brought them to a gopher hole. We dug out the top of the hole with a knife to a depth of about seven inches and a diameter of five inches. This was to make a kind of funnel into which to pour the water. Garter-snake emptied one pail and I, the second. We each stood ready with a stick. We found two gophers in this hole and killed them both. As they were dripping wet, we laid them in the sun near our fireplace to dry.

"Let us now shoot at a mark," said Stands-up. He took one of his wooden pointed arrows, thrust it by the feathered end into the ground, and upon the point stuck a small ball of horse dung. We went about thirty yards away. "Let us shoot two arrows each," said Stands-up. "Whoever hits the ball of dung shall have the two gophers we drowned out of the hole."

"You shoot first," said Garter-snake to me. I shot my arrows quite close to the mark. Garter-snake and Stands-up shot, neither hitting the mark. The second round, Garter-snake shot first, Stands-up shot second, and I third. We used only sharp wooden arrows. As soon as one shot, he ran and picked up his arrow.

The third round, Garter-snake shot first, hitting the ball of dung the first time. "There," he cried, "I eat the two gophers." He disemboweled them and made ready to roast them. "Now," he said, "I will give you two boys one of the gophers to divide between you. But while I am roasting them, see if you cannot catch another, and I will have my share of it."

"Agreed," I cried. Stands-up and I filled the two pails at the pond, and listening a few moments, heard *w-s-s-s-s!*—the hissing bark of a gopher. We looked and spied the gopher; he dived into his hole.

"It may not be a deep hole," said Stands-up, as he emptied the smaller of the pails which he held. The gopher did not come up. Stands-up filled the hole with water from the larger pail and as the gopher dashed out, he killed it with a blow of his bow. Drowned from their holes, gophers were easy to kill as they came up with their eyes shut, no doubt on account of the water.

I took the dead gopher to Garter-snake. "Here is the gopher you wanted," I said. "Good," he answered. "Now you roast it." I did so, and he said, "We agreed to divide this gopher, but I think it would be better if we shot again for it." "Agreed," said Garter-snake. "Whoever shoots the farthest shall eat this gopher." "Then I shall eat it," laughed Stands-up, as he shot. I followed, but my arrow failed to fly as far as his.

Garter-snake took up his bow. "I am sorry," he said, "that your arrows did not go farther. Now watch me!" He had a sinew-backed bow. He put an arrow on the string, drew it, and though he aimed at a rather low angle, his arrow went farthest of the three. We had shot with wooden pointed arrows.

"Now," said Garter-snake, "this is my gopher; but I am going to divide it with you, only I will take the chest, the best part. You boys may eat the back part. I don't like it anyway." We divided the gopher, Garter-snake eating the forequarters, and Stands-up and myself the hindquarters.

It was now about three o'clock in the afternoon. Other boys who had been herding their horses some distance away now came up, and we had a sham battle on horseback. We used roundheaded, or blunt, arrows. In the group were about ten boys, all of about the same age as my companions and I. Butterfly and Fingernail, I remember, were two of the boys.

We practiced fancy riding. One boy would ride along, dismount, and mount again, at a gallop. Another boy stood with his bow ready; a second boy galloped up near him, dropped on the farther side of his horse and swerved past, while the boy with the bow shot at the rider's horse.

Sometimes I galloped up to a boy, hidden behind my horse with only my leg exposed over the pony's back. The boy could see nothing but this exposed leg as I approached him. I struck him as I would an enemy; but as I galloped away, he shot at me, as he was now able to see my body. Of course, as I galloped away my horse turned, exposing my body to the other boy's arrow.

The easiest way to mount a horse (with no saddle) is to put the left elbow forward over the back of the horse, seize the horse's mane with the right hand and leap up, lying on the abdomen transversely over the horse's back; then throw the left leg over and rise to a sitting position. In battle we could not be so deliberate, as we ran the risk of being shot at by the enemy. We boys, therefore, practiced leaping from our ponies and mounting them again at a gallop. Seizing the mane with the right hand, one leaped from the right front, with the left foot lifted high, and vaulted onto the horse's back at one bound.

Then we played that I was thrown from my horse, or that my horse had been killed; and another boy rode forward to save me, carrying me of on his pony with him. The rescuer stopped his pony; I ran forward, placed both hands on the horse's hips and leaped up behind the other, very much as white children play leapfrog. Being trained to this, the horse did not kick. All these games were intended as preparation for battle, for all the boys expected to go to war, as they grew older. In these pony games I always rode my old gray mare.

We next practiced archery for a long while, using our bows again, as we thought we would do in battle. We put a stick in the ground and shot at it, just to see who was the best shot; or we took turns, each boy running forward, stopping suddenly, and shooting instantly. Very often a boy dashed past the mark, shooting at it as he ran. Sometimes the boys shot at one another; being careful, however, not to shoot hard. The boy who was the target tried to dodge the arrow, springing to right or left, or dropping suddenly so that the arrow passed by, or over, him. Only blunt arrows were used, at a distance of twenty or thirty yards. We practiced dodging arrows, because we expected to have to do so in war.

Of course, we guarded our horses all the time of our play, keeping our saddle horses close by and in readiness for any emergency. No matter what our play, we watched our herd and had our saddle horses ready.

We now mounted our horses, drove the whole herd to the river and watered them. I cut out my bunch of horses from the herd, the other boys cut out theirs, and we all returned to the village, arriving a little before sundown.

I drove my horses to my father's door, dismounted, and went in. My father was lying on his bed. "Are all the horses here?" he asked.

"They are outside," I answered.

"Good, I will attend to them," he said.

The other members of the family had already eaten their evening meal. I spread my blanket on the earth floor between the two forward main posts of the lodge and my mother brought me my supper in a wooden feast bowl, with a big Rocky Mountain sheep horn spoon to eat with. The mess was hominy of pounded yellow corn, boiled with beans, and seasoned with spring alkali salt, gathered from the edge of a spring. It was a dish that I liked.

TIPI LIFE: Like a coyote pup at the edge of its den, this little Cheyenne girl is ready to bolt inside if danger threatens. In this case it looks like the photographer already gave her a lollipop, so she's willing to stand and pose at the entry to her family home. Tipi children were taught to be wary of strangers and to remain still if anything unknown threatened.

Childhood Memories of Willie Eagle Plume

(Told at the Hungrywolf kitchen table in 1975).

I am Atsitsina (Prairie-owl Man), a Blood Indian, born in "the year the mountain fell" [1903, when part of a mountain came down—known as Frank Slide—burying the town of Frank, Alberta not far from the Blood Indian Reserve]. I was born in the old Indian way, although I have learned a lot of the white man's way since then.

My father was called Eagle Plume, because he once stole a prized racehorse from an enemy camp, and this horse had an eagle plume tied in its hair. My father took more than ten scalps from enemies on his war trails. He was one of the leading warriors in our tribe, and I grew up feeling proud to be his son.

When I was born, my father was also known as Natosina, or "Sun Chief". It was a name he inherited from a great medicine man of his own young days. By this time my father was a medicine man, too. The war and buffalo days had ended about twenty years before. We were at peace, and my father spent a lot of his time praying for people, doctoring them, and leading religious ceremonies for the tribe. My mother helped him with his work, and so did his other two wives; all three were related.

Because my father had several wives, I now have a brother who is only six months older. His name is Fred Eagle Plume, though in Blackfoot we know him by the name "Earth". His mother was my dad's first wife. She married him while still a young and pure girl, so she was allowed to put up the Medicine Lodge, or Sun Dance ceremony. My mother, Sikskiaki (Black-Faced Woman), could not do this with him because she had been married earlier. Her first husband, Low Horn, was killed when his wagon overturned and trapped him in a puddle of water. My mother, and her children from him, were able to escape. They had been on the way to a Sun Dance.

As I said, I was proud to be Eagle Plume's son—other people treated me with respect on account of my father, and their kids envied me. But my father did not spend much time with me. His work was very serious, and there were a lot of rules and regulations he had to follow. Kids are good at breaking rules, so we were not much allowed around him when he was busy. Instead, his mother—my grandmother, Otsani—took care of me a lot of the time. She was my real hero.

My grandmother still used a travois on her horse when she traveled around. By this time, most of the people in our tribe had wagons; some even owned those fancy buggies with fringe on top. But she liked her old horse and travois. I rode them both, and I liked them, too.

Grandma's horse was an old gray mare, and she used it mostly to go down in the river bottom for firewood and water. She used to bundle me up in a blanket and tie me on top of the little frame she built with thin poles over her travois. I was quite small at this time, but I still recall the strange, bumpy rides, looking backward, while my grandmother was leading the horse ahead. Sometimes my brothers and cousins were tied on with me, and we would make too much noise for the old lady, so she'd tell us to shut up.

But I was Otsani's pet, and she never got angry at me, even if I was with the crowd that woke her up when she was napping, or played tricks on her, like tying the laces of her moccasins together while she was asleep, or nailing her front door shut from outside! Sometimes we tied the legs of her old horse together, and she'd have a hard time figuring out why it wouldn't go. She was in her eighties and couldn't see too well anymore.

Sometimes a bunch of us kids would go down into the bushes with Otsani to help her gather wood and pick berries. After the work we would go swimming, while the old lady took a rest. She used to call me to her while the others were still playing, and she would unbraid and comb my hair. All the boys of that time wore their hair long—just like our fathers. She used a brush made from a porcupine's tail, dried, with a stick inserted for a handle. She made me feel very special at those times—I still get a very good feeling by thinking about them.

I wore a breechcloth all the time when I was small. I didn't know anything about store-bought underwear. My grandmother made breechcloths for me from soft buckskin she had tanned herself. She also made moccasins for me from the same thing. The leggings that I remember best were made from a white woolen blanket with colored stripes. She made them so that the stripes matched on both leggings and ran crosswise down my lower legs. Compared with the jeans and shirts I wear now, these old-time Indian clothes sound uncomfortable. The leggings were always coming untied from my belt and slipping down on one side or the other. The breechcloth could be even more awkward. But I don't remember getting cold on the exposed parts of my body, nor worrying about being awkward. It was all I had then, and I enjoyed my childhood.

My favorite shirt at that time was one my grandmother cut and sewed for me, by hand, out of a large flour sack. It was soft and warm, but the best part was the horned head of an elk printed in color on both sides, along with a bunch of fancy writing. The shirt was made so that the elk heads were on my chest and back, and I sure was proud of them. I guess it was an early version of those decorated shirts young people wear nowadays!

My coat was made from a blanket, in the style of capotes first seen on French trappers, who came into our country in the early 1800s. It had no pockets, but a long, pointed hood hung down behind. In this hood I used to stash my goodies, including the treats my grandmother gave me to eat while I was out playing—mostly bits of dried meat and berries; and sometimes, candy from the trading posts.

My father always had lots of horses, so I've been riding all my life. Otsani started to put me on the back of her old gray mare when I was three or four. That horse was so gentle, kids could play around its legs and not bother it at all. Young kids were often tied to saddles on the backs of tame horses like this, and left for hours at a time, while the animal grazed at the end of a rope. I've seen kids fall asleep right in the saddle while "riding" like this.

Among my favorite childhood toys were bows and arrows. I had several sets of them, since they were forever getting lost and broken. Mostly, my father made these for me, or else they were presents from various uncles. Since we boys had no money for betting with, in our various games and races, we often used arrows and sometimes bows.

My father made the last bow I ever had, and this one stayed with me until after I was married. It was a real work of art, with sinew backing and snakeskin covering. It sure was powerful! I sometimes earned a little money in my teenage years by giving demonstrations with this bow and arrows at rodeos and fairs.

We learned to shoot our bows and arrows by hunting gophers and small birds, less often by shooting at "marks," such as tree stumps. The arrows for such shooting did not have tips, and sometimes they even lacked feathers. A father who was really fond of his little son might make him feathered arrows to use for practice, but these were eagerly sought by the older boys in betting contests! The fanciest arrows a boy of my time could own were feathered ones that were decorated right up the shaft by spiral lines. To make these, a man would peel each arrow in a long spiral, leaving behind half the bark. Then he would grease the shafts and hold them over a smoky fire until they turned dark brown. Then he would peel off the remaining bark, revealing a light spiral.

A lot of the games we played as boys would have made us tough for battle, except that the warpath days were over. Often we divided into two groups and attacked each other with dried manure, sometimes kicking or wrestling each other to the ground in the process. We did a lot of wrestling, including what is often called "Indian wrestling", where two lie on their bellies, face each other, lock hands, and try to push each other's arms down.

We didn't know much about boxing, except as a white man's "sport". Our fighting was not meant for sport, but to prepare us for battle. We kicked each other to see who was toughest, and we even shot at each other with blunt-tipped arrows. The only thing the older people told us was to treat each other with respect, even when fighting. Bullies, and ruffians who actually caused trouble were unpopular among us.

A popular game for boys of my time involved the throwing of knives, or sometimes awls. Two of us would take turns throwing a knife into the ground so it would stick, each throw being a little harder. We'd start out by throwing the knife with each pair of our fingers, until we'd gone through both hands. After that, we'd stand the tip of the knife on the ends of our fingers, one at a time, making it stick into the ground. Whenever the knife didn't stick, the other fellow won. In real exciting games we'd get so far that we'd stand the knife up on our heads and make it spin down before it stuck in the ground. Sometimes a boy would end up sticking himself with a knife, then he would run home crying, and the rest of us would scatter to avoid trouble.

We used to imitate the older boys, and especially the men, who told their stories of adventure around evening fires. Some of the kids had little tipis, and in them we would play "house". The boys would go out hunting for small animals, while the girls fixed up the homes and made fires. They would cook whatever we managed to shoot with our simple arrows, while we sat to one side, smoked miniature pipes, and told about our hunts If we had no luck with hunting, we'd go on the "warpath" and raid dried meat where someone wasn't looking—often from our mothers' food bags!

Even religious ceremonies were imitated in our childhood playing. The men and women in our tribe have always had sacred societies, so we made up our own, duplicating the regalia with whatever we could find. We made sacred staffs and headdresses, decorating them whatever feathers and bits of cloth we could find. Keep in mind that we never made fun of these things; we always had the respect taught by our parents for anything to do with prayers.

Still, I recall one thing I did as a teenage boy that must have taken me close to the border of disrespect. Since I was the daring one in our crowd, someone once said I should imitate the grown men by giving an important offering "to the Sun" during our Sun Dance celebration. Men sometimes gave weapons, prized clothing or even bits of their own bodies to show courage and humbleness.

This was in about my twelfth or fourteenth summer, during that time of the year when most of the tribe came together for an old-time tipi camp. The sacred lodge for the Sun had been ceremonially put up, and all that day the grown men had made offerings, and told the people of their greatest adventures. In the old days this was done to make everyone in the tribe proud and courageous, especially the boys and young men.

It was the last night of the big camp, and the moon was shining brightly. I wanted to impress the other boys with my offering, but I had nothing that seemed worthy of notice. Instead, I got my brothers to help me in rolling off a fancy new buggy that was parked behind someone's unpainted tipi. We brought it to the sacred lodge, where others were watching to see what I would do. Slowly, I took the buggy all apart, tying each of its pieces to the sacred lodge's special Center Pole. There I called out, like the grown-up men, but in a soft voice, "Here, Sun. I'm giving you this to show you how much I think of you," and so forth. I went on like that until I had the whole buggy hanging up.

The next morning, everyone got up early to pack their camps and head back home. That's when we heard the camp announcer walking around saying, "You people, that old man, White Owl, has lost his carriage. Please be on the lookout for it." So it wasn't long before someone brought this old man the report, "Your buggy is all in pieces, hanging up in the Sun Lodge!"

My, he sure was upset, calling us "dog faces" and other mean things that were our version of swear words. He had to go and pray hard to the Sun and explain why he was taking his buggy back. Some men helped him put it back together after that. I was sure scared somebody would tell on me, and I never pulled a trick of that sort again!

Even winter was a lot of fun when I was a little kid. My father made me a real old-time sled, except that he used beef ribs, instead of those from buffalo. It was just a little thing, but it sure went fast down the hills by our house. The ribs were tied together with rawhide, and a small piece of hide was stretched across to make a seat. It was my prized winter toy until some years later, when I got a big white man's sled from town.

Soon after I learned to ride by myself—when I was about six or seven—my father gave me a horse of my own! It was a little pony that grew up right around our house, just like a dog. It was so used to us children that we could wrestle with it or play around, and it never caused trouble. This horse and I must have learned about riding from each other at the same time. I used to race it and have imitation battles against my friends, while pretending it was my war pony. Sometimes another boy would get on the horse with me, and we would challenge another pair, also riding a pony, to see who could drag the other off his mount.

At about that time, I started going to school, down at the Stand-off Day School, so I rode there on my pony. That was when my long hair got cut, and I began wearing store-bought clothing—"white man's dress", we called it. My father did not like the change in our appearance, but he encouraged my brother and me to learn well in school, mainly so that we'd "learn to get around among white men without being cheated," he would say.

I had a good time at this school, and I learned a bit about life during the few years I went there. I have heard about Indian children who were treated very badly in schools; even my own children were disciplined very strictly at the Catholic boarding school on our reserve. But my schooling was not so harsh, at all. Don't forget, the Bloods always defended their lands very fiercely and only settled on this reserve on their own agreement, after the buffalo died out. In my young days, our fathers were proud men who didn't let outsiders come into their home lives to push them around. This attitude has done a lot to make me sat-isfied in life, especially when I see how other people struggle.

At school, I may have looked like any Canadian kid, at least from the back. But at home our whole family still lived pretty much like old-time Indians. We had log houses and cook stoves, but our parents spent much of their time in tipis, and we kids spent most of ours out-doors.

When I was about eleven or twelve, I started breaking horses. My older "brothers" (including cousins, and so on) dared me to do it, and I was the kind ready to take them up on it. We picked out a yearling from my dad's herd, although we didn't go to him for permission. He would have said it was too dangerous, which is probably what his dad said to him. We looked for a slim and lively horse that showed signs of becoming a good runner. One of the older fellows rode his own horse and caught this one with a rope. We led it down over the embankment from the prairie to the river bottom, where we picked out a place with lots of deep mud. We led the horse out into the mid-dle of this, and that's when I sloshed my way next to it and somehow pulled myself up on its back.

The poor horse was pretty tense and nervous by this time, after being roped, pulled, and surrounded by a bunch of excited boys. It tried to buck me off, getting really frantic and throwing slobber with its head, but it couldn't do much with its legs down in the mud. I finally lost my grip on the mane, while all the others yelled for me to hold on longer. But when I fell, it was only into mud, from where I jumped up and got right back on the horse again. Eventually, the ani-mal was so tired that it no longer objected to my presence, at which point the others led us out on dry land, where we all paused for a few minutes, while the horse allowed me to sit still.

When my dad learned what I'd done, he didn't scold me; instead, he gave me the young horse for a present! Had I been hurt, then he would have scolded me!

After that, I began to get a reputation for breaking horses. Eventually, I quit school and began earning money by working with horses. I was still a teenager when I began competing against white cowboys in small-town rodeos. Sometimes I won a few dollars, other times I had to leave behind my winnings when bullies drove me out of town. I soon learned what my dad had meant about being cheated among the white men! Some were very good friends of mine, while others acted as if I were not much better than the horses in their corrals.

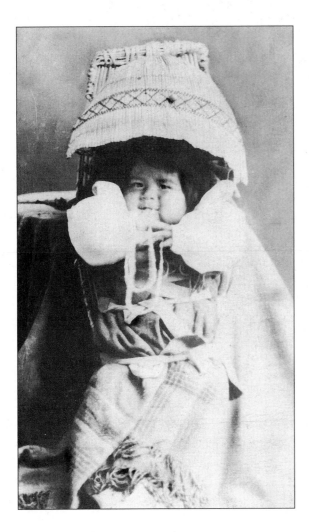

TIED UP IN SAFETY: This Paiute baby lived in the deserts of Nevada, about 1920. Protected by a sturdy cradleboard, whose basic frame is made of peeled willow sticks laced together to form the flat back frame and the curved head guard. The baby is wrapped in a fringed shawl then laced to the board with long buckskin thongs. Older babies like this sometimes get to have their arms and hands free.

The Debut of Aloyasius

(A 1920s boarding-school story by Estelle Armstrong, excerpted from *The Red Man*, student newspaper of the Carlisle Indian school in Carlisle, Pennsylvania)

The roofs of the buildings at the United States Indian school were painted red. Aloyasius could not remember the time when he had not watched their glittering surfaces, looming higher still, than the bare sun baked hill that had reared them, and which hid the muddy waters of the Colorado, as it eddied lazily between the dirty Arizona town and the reservation of his people.

At times, more often in the early morning, before the sun had dried the mists that hid the jagged mountaintops in clouds of coolness, the dazzling redness of the roofs softened, and their vivid glare blended tenderly with the lights and shadows of the dreary windswept landscape. But at noonday, when Aloyasius lay half-buried in the sand on the shady side of his father's mud hut, the glare of the almost tropic sun on their red expanse seemed to dissolve the color into flaming particles that scintillated dizzily in the waves of heat that rippled between him and the hill.

At such times, Aloyasius hated most the sight of the Government Indian school. He had always known that sometime he must go there, tho perhaps not till the Indian Agent had discovered that he was old enough. His brothers and sisters were already there and could speak the hated English. Aloyasius could not speak English. His brothers never spoke it when they came home on Sunday for the weekly half-holiday.

He knew, too, why he must go. His feeble old grandparents might not get their monthly rations, unless the children were sent in. So the Indian Agent had said, and the Indian Agent was to be feared and obeyed, above all else. Then, too, there was often no food in the mud hut—never was there enough—and children must be fed. At the Government school there was plenty, with meat daily and clothes to wear, and yet Aloyasius rebelled savagely. In his stolid, childish way, he resisted the fate that was forcing him under the shadow of those glaring red roofs.

Now the day had come. His father had gruffly bidden him, "Catheca"; and so he left the mud hut and followed his father along the narrow path that wound in and out among the rank arrow-weed that thrust out its pale spiny branches to entangle his bare legs, and up the steep graveled path to the school. At the door of one of the buildings, a woman was standing. To her, his father had given him.

Aloyasius knew she was a woman, because of her clothes, though neither she nor they were like anything that he had ever seen. At her hair, he marveled greatly. Perhaps it was that color because she lived under the red roofs. It was the color of them at evening, when the hot sun had set behind the western mountain peaks and the tender touch of twilight mellowed and made beautiful the things that glared by day. Aloyasius decided that it was pretty, but not pretty for hair. He liked hair that hung straight and black to one's waist, as his father's did, and tied with strings of many colors.

Strange as the woman looked, she did things still more strange. She took him into a room where a big tub stood in one corner and she filled the tub with clear, cool water. To Aloyasius, water—clear water like this, not muddy, as it came from the river—was something infinitely precious and not to be wasted. The women of his people carried it on their heads down the steep path from the school, in the large tin cans that the school cook gave them after they were emptied of their contents of syrup; and only at times, had he been allowed to drink all he wanted.

But, this woman took off his shirt—Aloyasius nearly always wore his shirt; only when the sun was hottest did he go quite naked—and made him understand that he was to get into the tub of water. His black eyes widened with fear, and he looked at the woman doubtfully. It must be the color of her hair that made her do such strange things, he thought. He obediently climbed in, and she took a cloth and something smooth and slippery that made a white foam when she rubbed it, and washed him. She got the white foam in his eyes and mouth and that smarted, but Aloyasius was too surprised to mind. The amazing idea of being washed, all over, stampeded all other emotions, for the first time.

She let him wipe himself dry and showed him how to put on the new clothes—the things which stuck so close to his skin—then a shirt and a pair of long khaki pants, like the ones the Indian police wore. Aloyasius revered and envied the Indian police, with their short gun at the hip and their belt with cartridges all around. She had only a comb in her hand when she returned, and she made him sit down, while she combed the "neeill" out of his hair.

Aloyasius knew very well that there were "neeill" in his hair. There always had been; and he supposed they belonged there and accepted them without questioning, as he had the thirst and poor food, and the stones that bruised his bare feet. That these things could be remedied, had never occurred to him, nor to his people. But this woman combed his head till it was clean, and stopped it with kerosene. He was troubled, though already he knew that this woman with the strange hair, who had so suddenly shot into his little Yuma orbit, would do him no harm. Her touch was much kinder than his mother's, who left him to do much as he pleased, as long as he tended the one poor pony and stoned away the dogs from the family meal, as it cooked in a kettle over the open fire.

When the dinner bell sounded, Aloyasius went with the other children to the dining room. There, they sat on stools at tables, and a man tucked a white cloth under his chin. He had no idea why the cloth was put there; but, as all the other boys had them on, he concluded that it was still another strange article of clothing. It kept unfastening and slipping into his lap, and he wondered why it didn't go on with buttons as all the other clothes did. Poor little Aloyasius! He wondered over so many strange things that his brown head was fairly dizzy, and his brain felt as though it was done up in curl papers.

He tried to use his spoon and fork to eat with, as the man had told him, but they got in his way, and he was still hungry when the gong sounded, and the children took off the pieces of white cloth and folded them beside their plates. Aloyasius did the same, wondering the while why anything should be worn for so short a time. He wore his shirt at home for weeks and weeks, without thought of any change. But they did strange things under these red roofs. The roofs had come to be typical to him of the many clothes with the many buttons, which all wore who lived under them.

Aloyasius soon learned that the long pants and shirt were his play clothes, and when the bell rang after dinner was over—it seemed to him that the bell was always ringing for him to unbutton one set of clothes and button another—the woman had given him a pair of short black pants that stopped above his knees and fitted his round limbs so closely that they seemed to have grown on him. They were very tight, and when he bent over to lace the stiff new shoes, something happened to the pants behind. The women made him take them off and sewed the rent with strong thread. Then one of the boys told him to sit down to lace his shoes, and not bend over again.

Aloyasius was eagerly curious at school, watching the many wonderful happenings with uncomprehending eyes. There was another woman here, only she had black hair more like his own, and Aloyasius decided that he liked her better than the woman with hair like the roofs, who made him change his clothes so often and wash his face and hands many, many times a day. The "why" of the numberless unfamiliar occurrences was fast enveloping him in a cloud of distrust and doubt. Why must he wash and wear so many clothes and eat with pointed things, instead of his fingers? Aloyasius thought, if only he could know why these things had to be, he would do them much more cheerfully.

When school was over, he had to change from his school clothes to his play clothes, before he could go out to play. Then came supper, with the white cloth that wouldn't stay on; then more play, and then to bed. Aloyasius was not accustomed to elaborate ceremonies attending his retirement for the night, and the sight of so many narrow white beds, side-by-side in a big room with wide, iron-barred windows, made him open his eyes in astonishment. The tightening in his throat caused him to catch his breath with a sob. The woman showed him where he was to lie, and helped him off with his clothes—all his clothes this time—even those that stuck so close to his skin, and gave him a long, loose thing, like a girl's dress, to put on. Aloyasius found when he struggled into it, that it had buttons on the back, and he wondered with all the powers that the long day of wonderment had left to him, why going to bed under the red roofs was so very different from going to bed in his father's hut.

His brother had told him in his own tongue that he must get down and say his prayers before he got into bed, and Aloyasius stood uncertain, not knowing quite how to go about it. He had oftentimes gone to the little Mission on the reservation and had learned to kneel at certain times, but to kneel at night before you went to sleep was queer. He crept between white sheets and lay very still. His heart ached for his corner in the sand at home, where he curled up at night with his mother's gay shawl, or his father's coat, thrown over him. He drew the despised government blanket over his throbbing head and cried his little heart out beneath the shelter of the glaring, red roofs.

The Return

(By Estelle Armstrong, from *The Red Man*, student newspaper of the Carlisle Indian School in Carlisle, Pennsylvania, 1925)

The old squaws, sitting squat on the platform beside their mounds of beadwork, looked at Jose as he swung himself from the day coach of the Overland, and nudged each the other in derision of his uniform and close-cut hair. Sitting there with their cheap, gaudy strings of beads held up to catch some unwary tourist's eye, their hair long and dank over shapeless, ugly shoulders, grimy faces impassive with the expressionless stare of the hopeless, the old women seemed to be the very spirit of ridicule incarnate, against which nearly every student is pitted, on return from school to his reservation home.

The innate hatred of the older Indians for the white man's dominating activity, with its resulting absorption of their own purposeless lives, eggs them on to use the only weapon left them in retaliation, often undoing by their witless ridicule of returned students what years of study and careful training have inculcated. For, you may beat an Indian in a fair fight, and he will respect you. You may cheat him in a horse trade, if you can, and he will be wary of you. But, expose him to ridicule before his peers, and he is your enemy forever. Ridicule of his person is one thing that nature has not fitted an Indian to bear.

The evil potency of this enervating criticism is recognized by every educator of our Indian youth who has watched the returned student conquer, or be conquered by, it. Because this spirit of ridicule is not an attribute of any particular tribe or locality, but is common to every clan: of valley, mountain, or barren plain, I select the homecoming of Jose as typical of many such that I have witnessed; and having witnessed, marveled, not at the half-failure sometimes resulting, but at the optimism that dared to expect success.

Jose was but an indifferent student at best, mastering the intricacies of the sixth grade in his nineteenth year, the fifth and last of his term at Carlisle. Balanced against his poor classroom record, were his good conduct as a student, his industry in the workshop, and his ability as an officer of Company C. In fact, he was an average student among the full bloods; who, as a rule, do not take kindly to books and abstruse problems, but with their hands do well and faithfully what is given them to do.

He had been 14 years old when he left the hot Arizona reservation on the Colorado, and the five years had wrought many changes in the dark-skinned boy who, at nineteen, walked with head and shoulders erect and saw that his shoes were duly polished, his clothes and nails immaculate. At age fourteen, Jose had a slouching posture; shoes were unknown, and clothes were a concession to encroaching civilization that he had detested.

Of his early home life, he had but confused memories. He had received no word from his parents in those five years. The remembrance of the squalor and meanness of earlier times faded from his mind, and his thoughts of home were a misty background of idleness and freedom, against which his present life loomed portentous and grim.

And now, the same forceful hand which had so deliberately taken him from his home five years before, was calmly replacing him in the groove that nature had fitted him for, after having done all in its power to make him unsuited for it. If Jose had been given to ponder on the reason of things, he might have questioned the wisdom that had separated him from his natural environment to teach him customs and habits that rendered that same environment detestable—only to return him to it. Happily, Jose had no such questioning. He was going home—home to his kindred and early playmates—to the misty memories of his boyhood home.

Home! He had come to it at last, with the tropical sun beating down upon him and a strange sinking in his heart at the sight of the leering squaws at the station.

He gripped his suitcase and elbowed his way through the crowded platform, thronged with travelers, Mexicans and men of his own tribe. The latter wore corduroys and light shirts, their long hair bound at the neck with gay kerchiefs and decorated at waist and elbow with strips of calico of many colors. They turned to stare at him, insolently noting his smart uniform, his cropped hair, and his general well-groomed appearance, breaking into loud guffaws at his expense as he passed them. Among their number were two of Jose's early playmates, with whom he had swum the eddying Colorado in former days, sounding each treacherous sandbar and skirting dangerously close to the seething whirlpools; but he passed them now with no sign of recognition. They failed to understand that one of his boyish anticipations of homecoming had vanished in their chorus of rude laughter.

As he climbed the steep hill that skirted the Colorado and hid from view the reservation of his people, Jose felt his pulses bounding rapidly. He had not expected his parents to meet him at the train. They were very old—had been old when Jose left five years before—and had many sons, of which he was the youngest. Without thought, he took the old path leading to his father's hut. The dust lay like a powder on every bush and shrub, stinging his eyes and throat. He found himself wondering if this father's home was like the open, grass-thatched hovels that he passed, around which naked children stopped their play to stare at him, and mongrel dogs challenged from a safe distance. His uncertain memories of home had been largely of the freedom and unrestraint of former years. They had dealt kindly with the poor hut and deprivation that had also been his portion.

An old woman raised her head from the pot of soup she was tending over a small open fire, and watched him as he approached. Jose recognized his mother. Old and bent with many years, her hair matted above her sunken eyes, her only garment a shred of filth that stopped above her knees, her inhuman hands ending in talons, the mother sat, and watched her son draw near. The accents of his native tongue came instinctively to Jose's lips, and he spoke hesitatingly, "mother". The sunken eyes lighted as she bent near, that her dim vision might view this stranger-son. Voiceless, the mother held him, and gazed long at his altered features and alien clothes.

Then, tottering to a prone form lying in the sand by the side of the hut, she spoke. Her words roused the wasted figure of Jose's father. With palsied hands, he shaded his eyes as he looked at his son. Rising slowly, and with difficulty, his raiment a loin cloth, and gray locks streaming over his shoulders—yet with dignity withal—he extended his hand in welcome.

As in a dream, Jose sat down on a nearby log and gazed about him. He saw the mean hut in its squalor and poverty; the heaps of rags in the sand on which his parents slept; the open fire over which hung the kettle of soup containing the coming meal; the sand and greasewood glaring in the July sun. He saw the Colorado with its treacherous, gleaming quicksand; and just beyond, the vicious frontier town, flaunting its vice so shamelessly. Then his gaze wandered back to the form of his mother, as she bent again over the pot of soup.

Four years had passed, and again the July sun beat down on the familiar scene. I looked from the car window as the Overland pulled in for a stop of ten minutes. We "took on water" here, and as I watched idly, I recognized in the stalwart figure running down the platform with a length of hose, our friend Jose.

Hastily making my way outside, I called to him. As soon as his work permitted, he came, doffing his cap and hesitating to give me his hand in greeting, soiled as it was from his recent labors. His overalls and working shirt were neat and whole, his hair closely cut and his face showed no signs of dissipation beneath its grime and sweat. He looked as I believed him to be: an honest youth engaged in honest work, and my heart rejoiced for him.

"Oh, yes," he replied to my question, "of course I am married. We have a child a year old and we are getting along just fine. I work over here at the railroad every day"; and he called, "Good-bye!", as our train got underway.

Consider, you who feel called upon to measure and to judge him by your standards, of which he falls so far short. Over against your pride of birth, your mother's prayers, the sense of honor inborn, your mental capacity of assimilation, I place the forms of Jose's parents, the squalor of the mud hut, the unbridled license of his early years, the frontier town with saloon doors always open, the pointing fingers of the leering squaws; and I challenge you to declare his education in vain, or to proclaim his life a failure.

Little-Joe's Back Home

(Ann Clark, *Little Boy with Three Names*)

All the morning noises of Taos were sounding together, telling the people that a new day was waiting for them.

Little-Joe opened one black eye. Sleepily, he looked up at the long, straight, white aspen poles that made a ceiling overhead. "Where am I?" he asked himself. "What is this place around me?"

His brown hand came out from underneath the bed-cover. It went feeling about on the wool-filled pad beneath him. "This is not my white bed. Where is my white bed and all the other white beds in this dormitory?"

"Little-Joe rolled over on his stomach. His head came out from the covers. It turned this way and that way. "I am just like a turtle looking out from my shell," he told himself, and laughed himself awake. Both black eyes were open now. They lighted up the slender brown face of the little Indian boy.

He knew where he was, now that he was all-awake. This was his mother's house. This was his bed on the floor of the family sleeping room. Beneath him was the mattress of soft wool that once had covered his father's sheep. He saw the good earth floor, hard-packed by walking feet.

Little-Joe stretched and stretched. Today summer began and he was in Taos again.

In the outer room he heard the soft footsteps of his mother as she moved about cooking breakfast for her family. He heard his older sister, Iao, playing with the baby. Iao's voice made little running sounds like water. The baby's laughter answered like the splash of a stone in the creek.

"I am the lazy one, to lie sleeping while my family move about me. I am new here. I have just come back from school."

Little-Joe sat up. He looked around for clothes to wear. Last night he had placed his school shoes side-by-side near the corner fireplace.

He had neatly folded his blue shirt and blue overalls, and placed them on a stool beside his shoes. Down there at the school, they had taught him that way. But now his clothes were gone. Deerskin moccasins stood where the school shoes had been. A calico shirt and beaded leggings were beside them. The little blue shirt and overalls, and the two school shoes were gone. There was no place in all this room for school clothes to feel at home. Everything here was new and strange to the little boy who had lived at Boarding School.

Everything here was Indian, for this place was Taos. It was the beginning of summer. Little Taos boys live in Taos in summer.

The Conversion of a Dozen Young Hopis

(Excerpt from the *New York American*, October 1912 issue)

The students mentioned in the following article left for their homes last July. Letters have been received from all of them, and the reports show that they are making excellent use of their education. One has opened a small store, several are employed at their mechanical trades, one is engaged in a trader's store, and the rest are farming. A fine spirit of service to their people is breathed in their letters, which show their emancipation from paganism and the old life of opposition to progress and education.

That a misunderstanding of the white man's motives has been one of the causes of the Indian's backwardness in adopting civilized methods, and of fighting education, is being demonstrated at the Government Indian School at Carlisle, Pa., where twelve members of the Hopi nation—sun worshipers and pagans—who went there five years ago virtually as prisoners of war, are now preparing to spread the doctrine of the new life that they have gladly accepted.

These twelve Hopi Indians, when they arrived there five years ago, were crude specimens. Long hair hung down their backs, they were garbed in discarded khaki uniforms and blue army overcoats, and none of them could speak a word of English. Now these same Indians,

HOPI BOYS WITH GRANDPA: The old man is shading his eyes, trying to look at the tourists who are aiming cameras towards his household. The ancient and picturesque villages of the Hopi people have long drawn the attention of outsiders, with Hopi youngsters used seeing cameras, and being bribed with candy or small change to pose for pictures. Yet in spite of this source of distraction the Hopi have continued to hand down a complex and wonderful ritual culture from one generation to the next, even to this day. At the time of this photo, circa 1910, Hopi children still wore traditional style clothing all the time, including their thick-soled style of desert moccasin, though the young boy in front is making himself tough by walking barefooted on the rough, hot ground.

The Hopi are among the Southwest's pueblo-dwelling people, whose homes were built with thick walls of adobe that kept homes cool in the summer and warm in the winter. The door at the right is a modern convenience—pueblo homes were traditionally entered through holes in their flat roofs, which were reached by pole ladders that could be pulled up incase of enemy attack. A pair of these poles are visible in the foreground shadow.

having gone through the white man's melting pot, are considered among the best students in the school, have renounced the sun and have joined Christian churches, are precise gentlemen in their conduct, and one of them has achieved international fame.

A half-dozen years ago, the Hopi nation was causing considerable trouble in Arizona. Internecine strife had divided the tribes, and a troop of United States cavalry was sent posthaste to the Keam's Canyon region to restore peace.

After powwows and conferences in which the Indian leaders sternly refused to adopt the white man's education, twelve of the most obstinate "stand patters" were taken as prisoners of war and sent from the Moqui Agency in Arizona to the Carlisle Indian School, the party arriving there January 26, 1907. All of these Indians were members of the Oraibi band of the Hopi nation. Among them were several priests and headmen of the tribe.

When these savages arrived at the Carlisle School they would have nothing to do with any of the other students, and began to live their lives apart. As they could speak no English, they expressed their thoughts by gestures and in garbled language.

In order to experiment, the authorities of the school did not order these Hopis to have their long locks of hair cut, but waited to see if their association with the advanced Indians at the school would not have some good effect upon them. In less than ten days, one of the Hopis indicated by gestures that he would like to have his hair cut like the other students, and on the same day another Hopi was discovered snipping off his own locks with a hunting knife.

From the moment the Hopis showed their first interest in education, they advanced rapidly and became eager in their desire to learn more. They entered the lowest grades in the classrooms, but as they were attentive to their studies, were kindly disposed to their teachers, and caused not the slightest trouble, they climbed to the top. All were assigned to devote some portion of their time to vocational training, some entering the blacksmith shops or carpenter shops; and Lewis Tewanima, the crack Marathon runner, developed into an expert tailor.

"These boys were ridiculed at first by the other students, it being a common habit of the aboriginal race," declared Superintendent Friedman. "But the newcomers persevered, until they were among the most respected and best-liked students in the school. The Hopis were absolutely converted to education and civilization. Where before they were sun worshipers, and the snake dance was one of their principal ceremonies, they have all joined Christian churches.

"When these Hopi boys return home they will be leaders among their people, and fight for both education and righteousness. Now all speak English, all read and write; they are courteous, and are gentlemen. They have kept in continual touch with their people, and already this influence has been noticeable in the Hopi country."

Lewis Tewanima, one of these same savages five years ago, is today the greatest long-distance runner in the world; and two years ago, while representing America at the Olympic games in Paris, won the main Marathon event. He represented this country at the recent Olympic games at Stockholm. Washington Talyumptewa has also achieved a national reputation as a long-distance runner.

Little Taos Boy at a Dance

(Ann Clark, *Little Boy with Three Names*)

At the campfire supper there was buffalo meat and bread and coffee for everyone. Tso'u had not tasted buffalo meat before, but he knew how it should taste. His grandfather had told him. He said to the man at the barbecue pit, "I would like the meat from the hump part. It is sweeter there." All the Indians laughed. Even Pachole laughed. Tso'u did not like it. He took his bread and meat and sat within the shadows.

After the Indians had eaten, they made ready for dancing. Pachole rebound his long hair, and Tso'u made his in a war-like roach, as his grandfather had taught him to do it. They put on their arm feathers and their fantail feathers. They put on their dance moccasins. They got their willow hoops and Uncle's drum.

Then they joined the long, long line of Indians. Those who lived nearer and had come on horseback were at the head of the line. They rode their horses forward slowly. Slowly, they rode them into the great oval plaza of the Indian Ceremonial grounds. Slowly, they walked them around the plaza and out again into the soft blackness of the night shadows. Then the line of men on foot moved forward. They moved forward into the Ceremonial plaza. There, three of the biggest campfires that Tso'u had ever seen were burning. Their great logs crackled and blazed, sending showers of little sparks up into the night sky. All the tribes of Indians were singing their own songs. Some men made little dancing steps and other men stepped high into the light of the fire flames.

At the front side of the dancing space there were seats. They were high like the houses of Taos. Many people were sitting there. You could see their faces in the darkness. You could hear their hands moving. You could feel their eyes looking at you. You could feel them liking you.

At the back of the dancing space were the standing Indians, their horses, wagons, shelters and their campfires.

The stars were crowded close together and they were hanging low.

The line moved on before the seats of the people. Tso'u made dancing steps. He was not afraid. He could feel his heartbeats in his fingers and in his toes. He knew that his arm feathers and his fantail feathers were shining in the firelight. He whispered to Pachole, "I am riding White Pony over the high places. The clouds are at my feet. Rain falls below me."

Now all the Indians were in the Ceremonial dancing plaza. They stopped walking. They grouped themselves at the back of the plaza. Then the different tribes danced their dances. Their chorus of singers sang for them and made them music with their rattles and drums and little bells.

Tso'u watched. He liked it.

Soon it was time for Taos dancing. All the faces out in the darkness were looking. The campfires flamed. Uncle sang the hoop dance song. Pachole and Tso'u danced. They turned their hoops this way and that way, and made their bodies go through them, like the music of Uncle's singing. They made their bodies like water, pouring through the hoops in a flashing stream. They stepped lightly, lifting their feet as the words of the song lifted high in the air.

Then it was finished. The hoop dance was finished. All the dances were finished.

The Indians went back to their campfires. Tired ones went to sleep in their blankets, but the old ones sang the stars to bed and the sun to a new day.

For three days and three nights, the Indians sang and danced and feasted together. On the morning of the fourth day the Ceremonial was over.

The Indians went back to their homes. On horseback and in wagons, in cars, on trains and buses, the Indians went home.

Ceremonial was over.

A Sun Dance Child of the Blackfeet

(Told by tribal elder Mike Swims Under in the Hungrywolf home in the fall of 1985)

My name is Mike Swims Under. My parents called me Many Stars, which is my Indian name. My father's name was Swims Under, but he was also called Chief Bird and Last Tail Feather. My mother's name was Mink Woman. She was a Holy Woman; she put up Sun Dance Lodges with my father. I grew up in the Sun Dances with them.

The first thing I remember about my parents is how devoted they were to our Blackfoot traditional customs and religion; they raised me to be devoted to them, as well. They brought me along to all the many ceremonies, including the Beaver Bundle and Medicine Pipe Dances, in addition to the Sun Lodge, which was the biggest event of all.

In Blackfoot, we say 'minpoka' to a child who is treated like I was—one who is taken to ceremonies among the tribe's leaders. In this way, I learned to respect the customs of my ancestors. I learned the songs and the ways of praying. I learned to love Nature and the Sun.

Life has changed a great deal on the Blackfeet Reservation since I was born, in 1913. But it changed a great deal in the time of my parents, too. My father was born before our people settled down; they were still living with the buffalo, which was a much different kind of life than we have now.

My father taught me the disciplines of our ceremonial ways, and there are many. I was given initiations so that I could take part. He warned me never to practice any of these ceremonials, or even sing their songs, unless I first got initiated. He said it would be harmful if I just made-up ceremonial things out of my own mind. Such things as songs, face paintings, and so forth, these have all been handed-down from dreams and visions of various people. They are not just made-up or imitated for style and show!

I was able to grow because of the breast. My mother fed me, and this was the way she gave me nourishment. She gave me part of herself. That is how it goes in nature; the children are fed from the bodies of their mothers.

When I got bigger, I remember receiving broths. That is how I was introduced to adult food. I also recall eating from the collection of fine crumbs that collected at the bottoms of my mother's rawhide parfleches. In them, she stored dried meat, berries, fat, dried roots, and mint. This mixture was my childhood delicacy.

My mother and father never whipped me, or even spanked me. They spoke sternly to me, and lectured me often, starting when I got old enough to reason. All the time that I grew up they kept after me, and that is how I turned out to be who I am.

THEIR OWN TIPI: Being raised in the wilderness and schooled at home gave my children a lot of experience in the kind of outdoor living practiced by their Blackfoot ancestors, even though it had been a full 100 years since the tribe settled on reservation lands, after the final buffalo hunts of the early 1880s. From left: Wolf, Okan, Iniskim, and sister Star.

I didn't always listen to my parents, as I grew older. The time came when I started smoking, then drinking moonshine liquor. My parents always told me what the consequences of my actions could do to my life. But they never hit me. I finally gave up drinking, when I saw that it kept me from enjoying my life and my prayers fully.

Now I work instead, to help the people of our tribe by setting an example in the Sun Lodge. There are enough initiated people so that we can still carry on with it, and some of them are quite young. I am now the leader for the ceremonies, and I try to do just what my father did when he was leader. It is sometimes very difficult for me, because there are no elders left with whom I can consult. My parents did not have this problem, but I am still doing my best.

When my parents were still children, everyone in the tribe took part in the Sun Dance, or Okan, and everybody believed in it. They all knew how to behave there, with respect.

It was still quite a bit like this when I grew up, although not so many people took a direct part anymore. Not so many learned the songs and got the initiations. The camps kept getting smaller, until finally we thought the Sun Dance and everything with it, was going to end forever.

But now, there are again many younger people who show faith in these ways. For a long time it was only old people, but now the young have come part of the way back to our own ways. They are at least trying to keep some of our ceremonies going. It should be up to the parents to teach their children about our customs and about the many rules and regulations. But most parents today don't know much about it, so some of the young people have a hard time to get good advice. The main thing is to have respect for all things, and lots of patience. You have to treat our way of life good, if you want it to help you.

Prayers, songs, and incense are powerful things to live on; they give you courage and good luck. Now that I am old, I can fully understand what my mother and father tried to tell me about faith and goodness. I'm following my ancestors, and I consider my life a holy way. I give thanks to the Sun and the Earth for letting me live. I give thanks for the Sunny Days and the Cloudy Days. I think all true prayers go to the same creator.

I encourage the young people to learn about the ways of their ancestors—the ways of living with respect for nature. It is easy nowadays, even the schools encourage it. In my time this was not so; the society of my time did not encourage us to be like Indians. In some of the mission schools they beat kids who showed interest in our customs, or who spoke the Indian language. They cut their hair right off, and tried to make white children out of them.

I was lucky; I didn't go to a mission school. My parents wanted me nearby them, so my father would not let me be taken away to boarding school. I attended a small day school near our home, instead. I have always lived close to the mountains, on our reservation, far from the towns.

Our school had ordinary government teachers, instead of nuns and priests, so things were more relaxed. My parents rented one of the little houses by the school, so they even lived near me in the daytime. Several families lived around there like that. It was somewhat like the old-time camps, except that we got government rations instead of having to follow the buffalo. Even so, my father did hunt for some of our meat, which my mother prepared in the old ways. We also grew a vegetable garden, which they learned to do from the white people. I have grown gardens for most of my life.

I am saddened when I see how many children today grow up in a very crazy life. Even their parents don't set good examples for them. Many don't care for their children, only for themselves. They hit their children and neglect them. The old people used to say, "When you hit a child, you knock them crazy." The more you hit them, it seems, the crazier they get.

But nowadays, there are children who don't get any discipline at all, not just hitting, and they are just as crazy. They only watch TV, and they copy what they see on it. Or they copy other kids who have copied the TV. It's all crazy, and it makes no sense to me. There is no prayer and no purpose to it. I'm glad whenever I see some of them returning to the ways of faith and prayer. Faith in life is what I've gotten from the ways that my parents taught to me.

Sioux boy all dressed up, circa 1910. His fully-beaded vest and moccasins, and partly-beaded buckskin pants, indicate that he was a favored child in a successful family.

SEVEN TALES FOR THE FIRESIDE

C hildren of the tribes loved to hear their people's stories by the fireside. In their simple, nature-oriented lives, storytelling was a major form of entertainment, not to mention the means for passing on tribal history, culture, and beliefs. Storytelling sessions were as important to traditional outdoor life as classroom lectures are in modern schoolrooms.

Children who showed early signs of learning the myths and tales of their ancestors were pointed out, by elders, as ones most likely to succeed in life. Noted storytellers were usually wise and creative, with much knowledge of medical and mystical things. They were skilled at relieving childhood ailments in several different ways. Yet, some of them were just plain good talkers.

Fireside storytelling sessions serve to stimulate a child's mind and ambition. Even today, children feel the magic of an open fire, as surely as all our ancestors felt it. What better time to tell stories and discuss the meaning of life? In the tribal past, legends introduced young listeners to dangers and hardships as challenges to overcome and goals to be proudly reached, rather than as fearful events to be dreaded. Can your children say that about the stories they hear, today?

Elders even gave their fireside listeners tests for courage. After a particularly hair-raising tale, an elder might ask a certain youngster to go out and fetch a pail of water. If there was a braggart or show-off in the bunch, he was sure to be chosen. Refusal meant ridicule in front of family and friends, so most youngsters bit their lips and rushed to the nearest source of water. Sometimes, if the elder felt the message had not been properly received yet by the child, he might spill out the water and say, "That was quick. Go get me some more!"

The stories presented here are but a few from the vast native collections that seem like the leaves of many trees. Fortunately, there are still native people committed to learning and passing on many of these tales, even with all the modern competition. This selection is merely presented to encourage your thoughts on this subject, in the hope that you'll take time out, now and then, to share tales and stories with the children who are around in your life.

Manitoshaw, the Hunting Girl

(Charles Alexander Eastman, *Indian Boyhood*)

It was in the winter, in the Moon of Difficulty (January). We had eaten our venison roast for supper, and the embers were burning brightly. Our teepee was especially cheerful. Uncheedah (my grandmother) sat near the entrance, my uncle and his wife upon the opposite side, while I, with my pets, occupied the remaining space. Wabeda, the dog, lay near the fire in a half-doze, watching out of the corners of his eyes the tame raccoon, which snuggled back against the walls of the teepee. Doubtless, his shrewd brain was concocting some mischief for the hours of darkness. I had already recited a legend of our people. All agreed that I had done well. Having been so generously praised, I was eager to earn some more compliments by learning a new one, so I begged my uncle to tell me a story. Musingly he replied:

"I can give you a Sioux-Cree tradition," and immediately began:

"Many winters ago, there were six teepees standing on the southern slope of Moose mountain, in the Moon of Wild Cherries (September). The men to whom these teepees belonged had been attacked by the Sioux while hunting buffalo, and nearly all killed. Two or three who managed to get home to tell their sad story were mortally wounded, and died soon afterward. There was only one old man and several small boys left to hunt and provide for this unfortunate little band of women and children.

"They lived upon teepsinna (wild turnips) and berries for many days. They were almost famished for meat. The old man was too feeble to hunt successfully. One day in this desolate camp a young Cree maiden—for such they were—declared that she could no longer sit still and see her people suffer. She took down her dead father's second bow and quiver full of arrows, and begged her old grandmother to accompany her to Lake Wanagiska, where she knew that moose had oftentimes been found. I forgot to tell you that her name was Manitoshaw.

"This Manitoshaw and her old grandmother, Nawakewee, took each a pony and went far up into the woods on the side of the mountain. They pitched their wigwam just out of sight of the lake, and hobbled their ponies. Then the old woman said to Manitoshaw:

"'Go, my granddaughter, to the outlet of the Wanagiska, and see if there are any moose tracks there. When I was a young woman, I came here with your father's father, and we pitched our tent near this spot. In the night there came three different moose. Bring me leaves of the birch and cedar twigs; I will make medicine for moose,' she added.

"Manitoshaw obediently disappeared in the woods. It was a grove of birch and willow, with two good springs. Down below was a marshy place. Nawakewee had bidden the maiden look for nibbled birch and willow twigs, for the moose loves to eat them, and to have her arrow ready upon the bowstring. I have seen this very place many a time," added my uncle, and this simple remark gave the story an air of reality.

"The Cree maiden went first to the spring, and there found fresh tracks of the animal she sought. She gathered some cedar berries and chewed them, and rubbed some of them on her garments so that the moose might not scent her. The sun was all ready to set, and she felt she must return to Nawakewee.

"Just then, Hinhankaga, the hooting owl, gave his doleful night call. The girl stopped and listened attentively.

"'I thought it was a lover's call,' she whispered to herself. A singular challenge pealed across the lake. She recognized the alarm call of the loon, and fancied that the bird might have caught a glimpse of her game.

"Soon she was within a few paces of the temporary lodge of pine boughs and ferns which the grandmother had constructed. The old woman met her on the trail.

"'Ah, my child, you have returned none too soon. I feared you had ventured too far away, for the Sioux often come to this place to hunt. You must not expose yourself carelessly on the shore.'

"As the two women lay down to sleep they could hear the ponies munch the rich grass in an open spot nearby. Through the smoke hole of the pine-bough wigwam, Manitoshaw gazed up into the starry sky and dreamed of what she would do on the morrow, when she should surprise the wily moose. Her grandmother was already sleeping so noisily that it was enough to scare away the game. At last the maiden, too, lost herself in sleep.

"Old Nawakewee awoke early. First of all, she made a fire, and burned cedar and birch so that the moose might not detect the human smell. Then she quickly prepared a meal of wild turnips and berries, and awoke the maiden, who was surprised to see that the sun was already up. She ran down to the spring and hastily splashed handfuls of the cold water in her face; then she looked for a moment in its mirror-like surface. There was the reflection of two moose by the open shore, and beyond them Manitoshaw seemed to see a young man standing. In another moment all three had disappeared.

"'What is the matter with my eyes? I am not fully awake yet, and I imagine things. Ugh, it is all in my eyes," the maiden repeated to herself. She hurried back to Nawakewee. The vision was so unexpected and so startling that she could not believe in its truth, and she said nothing to the old woman.

"Breakfast eaten, Manitoshaw threw off her robe and appeared in her scantily-cut gown of buckskin with long fringes, moccasins and leggings trimmed with quills of the porcupine. Her father's bow and quiver were thrown over one shoulder, and the knife dangled from her belt in its handsome sheath. She ran breathlessly along the shore toward the outlet.

"Way off near the island, Medoza, the loon swam with his mate, occasionally uttering a cry of joy. Here and there, the playful Hogan, the trout, sprang gracefully out of the water, in a shower of falling dew. As the maiden hastened along, she scared up Wadawasee, the kingfisher, who screamed loudly.

"Stop, Wadawasee, stop—you will frighten my game.'"

At last she reached the outlet. She saw at once that the moose had been there during the night. They had torn up the ground and broken birch and willow twigs in a most disorderly way."

"Ah!" I exclaimed, "I wish I had been with Manitoshaw then!"

"Hush, my boy; never interrupt a storyteller."

I took a stick and began to level off the ashes in front of me, and to draw a map of the lake, tile outlet, the moose and Manitoshaw. Away onto one side, was the solitary wigwam, Nawakewee and the ponies.

"Manitoshaw's heart was beating so loud that she could not hear anything," resumed my uncle. "She took some leaves of the wintergreen and chewed them to calm herself. She did not forget to throw, in passing, a pinch of pulverized tobacco and paint into the spring for Manitou, the spirit.

"Among the twinkling leaves of the birch her eye was caught by a moving form, and then another. She stood motionless, grasping her heavy bow. The moose, not suspecting any danger, walked leisurely toward the spring. One was a large female moose; the other, a yearling.

"As they passed Manitoshaw, moving so naturally and looking so harmless, she almost forgot to let fly an arrow. The mother moose seemed to look in her direction, but did not see her. They had fairly passed her hiding-place when she stepped forth and sent a swift arrow into the side of the larger moose. Both dashed into the thick woods, but it was too late. The Cree maiden had already loosened her second arrow. Both fell dead before reaching the shore."

"Uncle, she must have had a splendid aim, for in the woods the many little twigs make an arrow bound off to one side," I interrupted in great excitement.

"Yes, but you must remember she was very near the moose."

"It seems to me, then, uncle, that they must have scented her, for you have told me that they possess the keenest nose of any animal," I persisted.

"Doubtless, the wind was blowing the other way. But, nephew, you must let me finish my story.

"Overjoyed by her success, the maiden hastened back to Nawakewee, but she was gone! The ponies were gone, too, and the wigwam of branches had been demolished. While Manitoshaw stood there, frightened and undecided what to do, a soft voice came from behind a neighboring thicket:

"'Manitoshaw! Manitoshaw! I am here!'

"She at once recognized the voice and found it to be Nawakewee, who told a strange story. That morning a canoe had crossed the Wanagiska, carrying two men. They were Sioux. The old grandmother had seen them coming, and to deceive them, she at once pulled down her temporary wigwam, and drove the ponies off toward home. Then she hid herself in the bushes nearby, for she knew that Manitoshaw must return there.

"'Come, my granddaughter, we must hasten home by another way' cried the old woman.

"But the maiden said, 'No, let us go first to my two moose that I killed this morning, and take some meat with us.'

"'No, no my child; the Sioux are cruel. They have killed many of our people. If we stay here they will find us. I fear, I fear them, Manitoshaw!'

"At last the brave maid convinced her grandmother, and the more easily, as she, too, was hungry for meat. They went to where the big game lay among the bushes, and began to dress the moose."

"I think that, if I were they, I would hide all day. I would wait until the Sioux had gone; then, I would go back to my moose," I interrupted for the third time.

"I will finish my story first; then you may tell us what you would do," said my uncle, reprovingly.

"The two Sioux were father and son. They too, had come to the lake for moose; but, as the game usually retreated to the island, Chatansapa had landed his son, Kangiska, to hunt them on the shore, while he returned in his canoe to intercept their flight. The young man sped along the sandy beach and soon discovered their tracks. He followed them up, and found blood on the trail.

"This astonished him. Cautiously, he followed on, until he found them both lying dead. He examined them and found that in each moose there was a single Cree arrow. Wishing to surprise the hunter if possible, Kangiska lay hidden in the bushes.

"After a little while, the two women returned to the spot. They passed him as close as the moose had passed the maiden in the morning. He saw at once, that the maiden had arrows in her quiver like those that had slain the big moose. He lay still.

"Kangiska looked upon the beautiful Cree maiden and loved her. Finally, he forgot himself and made a slight motion. Manitoshaw's quick eye caught the little stir among the bushes, but she immediately looked the other way, and Kangiska believed that she had not seen anything. At last, her eyes met his, and something told both that all was well. Then the maiden smiled, and the young man could not remain still any longer. He arose suddenly, and the old woman nearly fainted from fright. But Manitoshaw said:

"'Fear not, grandmother; we are two and he is only one."

"While the two women continued to cut up the meat, Kangiska made a fire by rubbing cedar chips together, and they all ate of the moose meat. Then the old woman finished her work, while the young people sat down upon a log in the shade, and told each other all their minds.

"Kangiska declared by signs that he would go home with Manitoshaw to the Cree camp, for he loved her. They went home, and the young man hunted for the unfortunate Cree band during the rest of his life.

"His father waited a long time on the island and afterward searched the shore, but never saw him again. He supposed that those footprints he saw were made by Crees who had killed his son."

"Is that story true, uncle?" I asked eagerly.

"Yes, the facts are well known. There are some Sioux mixed bloods among the Crees to this day, who are descendants of Kangiska."

The Poor Turkey Girl

(Excerpt from Frank H. Cushing, *Zuni Folk Tales*, G. P. Putnam's Sons, New York, 1901)

Long, long ago, our ancients had neither sheep nor horses nor cattle; yet they had domestic animals of various kinds—amongst them, Turkeys.

In Matsaki, or Salt City, there dwelt at this time many very wealthy families who possessed large flocks of these birds, which it was their custom to have their slaves, or the poor people of the town, herd in the plains round about Thunder Mountain, below which their town stood, and on the mesas beyond.

In Matsaki, at this time, away out near the border of the town, there stood a little tumbledown, single-room house, wherein there lived alone a very poor girl. She was so poor that her clothes were patched and tattered and dirty. Her person, on account of long neglect and ill-fare, was shameful to look upon, though she herself was not ugly, but had a winning face and bright eyes—that is, if the face had been more oval and the eyes less oppressed with care. So poor was she, that she herded Turkeys for a living; and little was subsisted on from day-to-day, and perhaps now and then a piece of old, worn-out clothing.

Like the extremely poor everywhere and at all times, she was humble, and by her longing for kindness, which she never received, she was made kind even to the creatures that depended upon her; and lavished this kindness upon the Turkeys she drove to and from the plains every day. Thus, the Turkeys, appreciating this, were very obedient. They loved their mistress so much that, at her call, they would unhesitatingly come; or at her behest, go wheresoever and whensoever she wished.

One day this poor girl, driving her Turkeys down into the plains, passed near Old Zuni—the Middle Ant Hill of the World, as our ancients have taught us to call our home—and as she went along, she heard the herald-priest proclaiming from the house-top that the Dance of the Sacred Bird (which is a very blessed and welcome festival to our people, especially to the youths and maidens who are permitted to join in the dance) would take place in four days.

Now, this poor girl had never been permitted to join in, or even to watch the great festivities of our people, or the people in the neighboring towns; and naturally, she longed very much to see this dance. But she put aside her longing, because she reflected: "It is impossible that I should watch, much less join in the Dance of the Sacred Bird, ugly and ill-clad as I am." And thus, musing to herself, and talking to her Turkeys, as was her custom, she drove them on. At night, returned them to their cages round the edges, and in the plazas, of the town.

Every day after that, until the day named for the dance, this poor girl, as she drove her Turkeys out in the morning, saw the people busy in cleaning and preparing their garments, cooking delicacies, and otherwise making ready for the festival to which they had been duly invited by the other villagers. She heard them talking and laughing merrily at the prospect of the coming holiday. So, as she went about with her Turkeys through the day, she would talk to them, though she never dreamed that they understood a word of what she was saying.

It seems that they did understand, even more than she said to them, for on the fourth day, after the people of Matsaki had all departed toward Zuni and the girl was wandering around the plains alone with her Turkeys, one of the big Gobblers strutted up to her. Making a fan of his tail, and skirts, as it were, of his wings, blushed with pride and puffed with importance, he stretched out his neck and said: "Maiden mother, we know what your thoughts are, and truly we pity you; and wish that, like the other people of Matsaki, you might enjoy this holiday in the town below. We have said to ourselves at night, after you have placed us safely and comfortably in our cages: 'Truly our maiden mother is as worthy to enjoy these things as any one in Matsaki, or even Zuni.'

"Now listen well, for I speak the speech of all the elders of my people: If you will drive us in early this afternoon, when the dance is most gay and the people are most happy, we will help you to make yourself so handsome and so prettily dressed that never a man, woman, or child amongst all those who are assembled at the dance will know you; but rather, especially the young men, will wonder whence you came, and long to lay hold of your hand in the circle that forms round the altar to dance. Maiden mother, would you like to go to see this dance, and even to join in it, and be merry with the best of your people?"

The poor girl was at first surprised. Then it seemed all so natural that the Turkeys should talk to her as she did to them, that she sat down on a little mound, and leaning over, looked at them and said: "My beloved Turkeys, how glad I am that we may speak together! But why should you tell me of things that you full well know I so long to, but cannot by any possible means, do?"

"Trust in us," said the old Gobbler, "for I speak the speech of my people, and when we begin to call and call, and gobble and gobble, and turn toward our home in Matsaki, do you follow us, and we will show you what we can do for you. Only let me tell you one thing: No one knows how much happiness and good fortune may come to you if you but enjoy temperately the pleasures we enable you to participate in. But if, in the excess of your enjoyment, you should forget us, who are your friends, yet so much depend upon you, then we will think: 'Behold, this our maiden mother, though so humble and poor, deserves, forsooth, her hard life; because, were she more prosperous, she would be unto others as others now are unto her.' "

"Never fear, O my Turkeys," cried the maiden—only half trusting that they could do so much for her, yet longing to try—"never fear. In everything you direct me to do, I will be obedient, as you always have been to me."

The sun had scarce begun to decline, when the Turkeys of their own accord turned homeward, and the maiden followed them, light of heart. They knew their places well, and immediately ran to them. When all had entered, even their bare-legged children, the old Gobbler called to the maiden, saying: "Enter our house." She, therefore, went in. "Now maiden, sit down" said he, "and give to me and my companions, one by one, your articles of clothing. We will see if we cannot renew them."

The maiden obediently drew off the ragged old mantle that covered her shoulders and cast it on the ground before the speaker. He seized it in his beak, and spread it out, and picked and picked at it, and then he trod upon it, and lowering his wings, began to strut back and forth over it. Then, taking it up in his beak, and continuing to strut, he puffed and puffed, and laid it down at the feet of the maiden—a beautiful white embroidered cotton mantle. Then another Gobbler came forth, and she gave him another article of dress, and then another and another, until each garment the maiden had worn was new and as beautiful as any possessed by her mistresses in Matsaki.

Before the maiden donned all these garments, the Turkeys circled about her, singing and singing, and clucking and clucking, and brushing her with their wings, until her person was as clean and her skin as smooth and bright as that of the fairest maiden of the wealthiest home in Matsaki. Her hair was soft and wavy, instead of being an ugly, sunburnt shock; her cheeks were full and dimpled, and her eyes dancing with smiles—for she now saw how true had been the words of the Turkeys.

Finally, one old Turkey came forward and said: "Only the rich ornaments worn by those who have many possessions are lacking to thee, O maiden mother. Wait a moment. We have keen eyes, and have gathered many valuable things; as such things, being small, though precious, are apt to be lost from time to time by men and maidens."

Spreading his wings, he trod round and round upon the ground, throwing his head back, and laying his wattled beard on his neck; and, presently beginning to crouch, he produced in his beak a beautiful necklace. Another Turkey brought forth earrings, and so on, until all the proper ornaments appeared, befitting a well-clad maiden of the olden days, and were laid at the feet of the poor Turkey girl.

With these beautiful things she decorated herself. Thanking the Turkeys over and over, she started to go, and they called out: "O maiden mother, leave open the wicket, for who knows whether you will remember your Turkeys or not, when your fortunes are changed; and if you will not grow ashamed that you have been the maiden mother of Turkeys? But we love you, and would bring you to good fortune. Therefore, remember our words of advice, and do not tarry too long."

"I will surely remember, O my Turkeys!" answered the maiden.

Hastily, she sped away down the river path toward Zuni. When she arrived there, she went in at the western side of the town and through one of the long covered ways that lead into the dance court. When she came just inside of the court, behold, every one began to look at her, and many murmurs ran through the crowd—murmurs of astonishment at her beauty and the richness of her dress, and the people were all asking one another, "Whence comes this beautiful maiden?"

Not long did she stand there neglected. The chiefs of the dance, all gorgeous in their holiday attire, hastily came to her; and, with apologies for the incompleteness of their arrangements, though these arrangements were as complete as they possibly could be, invited her to join the youths and maidens dancing round the musicians and the altar in the center of the plaza.

With a blush and a smile and a toss of her hair over her eyes, the maiden stepped into the circle, and the finest youths among the dancers vied with one another for her hand. Her heart became light and her feet merry, as the music sped her breath to rapid coming and going, and the warmth swept over her face, and she danced and danced until the sun sank low in the west.

But, alas! In the excess of her enjoyment, she thought not of her Turkeys; or, if she thought of them, she said to herself "How is this, that I should go away from the most precious consideration to my flock of gobbling Turkeys? I will stay a while longer, and just before the sun sets I will run back to them, that these people may not see who I am, and that I may have the joy of hearing them talk day after day and wonder who the girl was who joined in their dance."

So the time sped on, and another dance was called, and another, and never a moment did the people let her rest; but they would have her in every dance, as they moved around the musicians and the altar in the center of the plaza.

At last the sun set, and the dance was well nigh over; when, suddenly breaking away, the girl ran out. Being swift of foot, more so than most of the people of her village, she sped up the river path before any one could follow the course she had taken.

Meantime, as it grew late, the Turkeys began to wonder and wonder that their maiden mother did not return to them. At last, a gray old Gobbler mournfully exclaimed, "It is as we might have expected. She has forgotten us; therefore is she not worthy of better things than those she has been accustomed to. Let us go forth to the mountains and endure no more of this irksome captivity, inasmuch as we may no longer think our maiden mother as good and true as once we thought her."

So, calling and calling to one another in loud voices, they trooped out of their cage and ran up toward the Canyon of the Cottonwoods, and then round behind Thunder Mountain, through the Gateway of Zuni, and so on up the valley.

All breathless, the maiden arrived at the open wicket and looked in. Behold, not a Turkey was there! Trailing them, she ran and she ran up the valley to overtake them; but they were far ahead, and it was only after a long time that she came within the sound of their voices; and then, redoubling her speed, well nigh overtook them, when she heard them singing a song.

Hearing this, the maiden called to her Turkeys—called and called in vain. They only quickened their steps, spreading their wings to help them along, singing their song over and over, until they came to the base of Canyon Mesa, at the borders of the Zuni Mountains. Then, singing once more their song in full chorus, they spread wide their wings, and fluttered away over the plains above.

The poor Turkey girl threw her hands up and looked down at her dress. With dust and sweat, behold! It was changed to what it had been. She was the same poor Turkey girl that she was before. Weary, grieving, and despairing, she returned to Matsaki.

Thus it was, in the days of the ancients. Therefore, where you see the rocks leading up to the top of Canyon Mesa, there are the tracks of Turkeys and other figures to be seen. The latter are the song that the Turkeys sang, graven in the rocks; and all over the plains along the borders of Zuni Mountains since that day, turkeys have been more abundant than in any other place.

Coyote and the Fawn's Stars

(Excerpt from Robert Young and William Morgan, *Coyote Tales*, Navajo Life Series, Bureau of Indian Affairs, Haskell Institute, Lawrence, Kansas, 1949)

Once Coyote was out walking.
He was walking in the forest.
He met a deer. She had her baby with her.

Coyote said, "Hello, my cousin.
What pretty stars your baby has

on his back.
I wish my children had pretty stars."

Deer said, "Your babies can have stars.
I will tell you.
This is what I do.

When my babies are very little,
I build a big fire.
The sparks from the fire make the stars.
You can do that for your babies.
Then they will have pretty stars, too."

Coyote was happy.
Now he knew what to do.
He wanted his babies to have pretty stars.
He gathered wood.
He made a big fire.
He put all of his children in the fire.
The sparks flew.
"Now they will have pretty stars," said Coyote.

He danced around the fire.
Soon he said to Deer,
"Have they been in the fire long enough?"
"Yes," said Deer.
She ran away laughing.

Coyote took his children from the fire.
They were burned. They were dead.
Coyote was angry.
He chased Deer.
Coyote still chases Deer, but he
        never catches her.

Coyote and Crow

(Robert Young and William Morgan, *Coyote Tales*)

One day Coyote was out walking.
He saw Crow.
Crow was holding his hat under his foot.
"What is under your hat?" asked Coyote.
"I have a bluebird under my hat," said Crow.
"Will you hold it for me a little while," asked Crow.
"I will hold it," said Coyote.
"Don't look under it," said Crow.
"Don't let the bluebird get away."
"I will hold it," said Coyote.
"I will hold it until you get back."

Crow flew away.
He flew behind a rock.
He could see Coyote, but Coyote could not see him.

Coyote looked all around.
He did not see Crow.
He looked at the hat.
"A bluebird," he thought.
"A nice bluebird.
Crow is gone.
I'll eat the bluebird."

He looked around again.
He raised the hat carefully.
He grabbed—but it wasn't
            a bluebird.
It was a cactus.

"Caw, caw, caw," said Crow from the tip of the rock.

Coyote was angry.

He sat down to pick the thorns out of his foot.

"Caw, caw, caw," said Crow again and flew away.

Blackfoot Legends: Napi and the Great Spirit

("Napi" stories excerpted from American Museum of Natural History, Anthropological Papers, vol. 2, New York, 1909)

There was once a Great Spirit who was good. He made a man and a woman. Then Napi came along. No one made Napi; he always existed. The Great Spirit said to him, "Napi, have you any power?"

"Yes," said Napi, "I am very strong." "Well," said the Great Spirit, "suppose you make some mountains." So Napi set to work and made the Sweetgrass Hills. To do this, he took a piece of Chief Mountain. He brought Chief Mountain up to its present location, shaped it up, and named it. The other mountains were called Blood Clots. "Well," said the Great Spirit, "you are strong."

"Now," said Napi, "there are four of us—the man and woman, you and I." The Great Spirit said, "All right."

The Great Spirit said, "I will make a big cross for you to carry." Napi said, "No, you make another man so that he can carry it." The Great Spirit made another man. Napi carried the cross a while but soon got tired and wanted to go. The Great Spirit told him that he could go, but he should go out among the people and the animals, and teach them how to live, and so forth.

Now, the other man got tired of carrying the cross. He was a white man. The Great Spirit sent him off as a traveler. So he wandered on alone. The man and woman who had been created wandered off—down towards Mexico, where they tried to build a mountain in order to get to the sky to be with their children; but the people got mixed up until they came to have many different languages.

Napi and the Elk Skull

One day Napi was going along, when he came to an elk skull on the ground. Inside of it were some mice dancing. Napi began to cry, because he wanted to go in and dance with the mice. The mice told him that he was too big to get in and dance, but that he could stick his head inside, and shake it, which would be the same as dancing. "However," they said, "whatever you do, you must not go to sleep."

So, Napi stuck his head into the skull; but he forgot and went to sleep, and while he slept, the mice chewed all his hair off. When Napi awoke, he could not get the skull off his head, so he went into the river and swam along, with the antlers sticking up out of the water.

In this way, he passed a camp of Indians. Then he made a noise like an elk. The people shot at him, went into the water and dragged him out; but when they had him on shore, they saw that it was Napi. They took a stone and broke the skull, that he might get his head out again.

Napi Makes Buffalo Laugh

Napi looked from Red Deer River over to Little Bow River. He saw some buffalo. He tied up his hair in knots, and crawled along on hands and knees. The sight made the buffalo laugh. One of them laughed himself to death, arid Napi butchered him.

Origin of Names Among the Cherokees

(A legend told by Sylvester Long for *The Red Man*, student newspaper of the Carlisle Indian School, Carlisle, Pennsylvania, ca. 1925)

Among the interesting legends of the Cherokees is the one concerning the naming of children after animals and birds.

Long ago, when all Indians belonged to one great family, the children were not named until they were old enough to kill a certain number of the animals after which they wished to be named. The larger and fiercer the animal or bird, the more sought was its name. Thus the bear, wolf, eagle, and hawk were considered very good names. Those possessing these names were supposed to be endowed with great skill and prowess as hunters and warriors.

During this period, there lived a young chief, Eg-wah Wi-yuh, whose greatest ambition was to be the father of a brave son—brave enough to earn the name of some fierce animal. At the birth of his first child, he was greatly disappointed to find that he was born blind. So grieved was he over his afflicted son, that for five days he neither ate nor drank anything; neither did he allow anyone to enter his tipi. On the fifth night he fell into unconsciousness, and while in this condition a large bird entered his tipi and carried him away.

He awoke to find himself sailing through the air on the back of a large bird. He had not been awake long, before he discovered that they were traveling toward the moon, which already appeared many times larger than he had before seen it. On reaching the moon, he was surprised to discover that, instead of being the planet that he thought it to be, it was in reality, a large opening in a thick black crust. After passing through the moon, he saw on the other side, men walking around with large holes in their heads instead of eyes. On regaining his faculties, he asked the bird what all this meant and where he was being carried.

He was told that he had died and his spirit was being carried to Guh-luh-lau-eeh—Happy Hunting Grounds—to be judged and sent back to the place they had just passed. The bird, on being further questioned, explained that this place was built by the Great Spirit and intended for the spirits of animals and birds, but owing to the cruel custom of killing animals for their names, the Great Spirit had sent a curse upon the Indians. He had given the animals the real Happy Hunting Grounds and driven the spirits of the Indians to the place that they had just passed, to have their eyes eaten out by the birds, and tormented by the animals they had wantonly killed on earth, for the sake of assuming their titles.

He was informed that they were on the way to Guh-luh-lau-eeh, the real Happy Hunting Grounds, where the chief of the animals and birds dwelt, which was reached by passing through the sun. The moon, he said, was for the wicked spirits of the Indians to pass through during the night, and the sun for the spirits of the animals to pass through during the day. The Great Spirit covered the earth with the black sheet long enough for the evil spirits to pass into their torment, and the white one long enough for the spirits of the animals and birds to pass into Guh-luh-lau-eeh, thereby producing day and night.

On passing through the sun, he was amazed at the beauty of the place. He was carried to the large wigwam of the Great Chief of the animal and bird kingdom. On discovering that his subject was not dead, but had merely fallen into a stupor, from which he had already recovered, he was greatly annoyed and ordered the bird to carry Eg-wah Wi-yuh to the fiercest animals of the kingdom, to be devoured and his spirit sent to the land of evil spirits, to be tormented by the animals and birds.

Wi-yuh asked if there was anything he could do to save himself. The Great Chief told him that, yes, there was one thing he could do to save himself, and that was to go back to the earth and abolish the custom of slaying innocent animals and birds for their names. He told Wi-yuh that, if he accomplished this one task, he would make him ruler of the animal and bird kingdom, and would give back to the spirits of the Indians Guh-luh-lau-eeh, and allow them to hunt as much as they wanted among all the animals and birds in that kingdom. He promised that, if the young chief would name his blind child after the first animal or bird he would see on looking from his tipi the next morning after returning to his home, instead of adhering to the old custom, and thereby set an example for the other Indians to follow, he would cause the child to gain its eyesight.

On returning to the earth, Wi-yuh told his people all that had happened and they did not believe him, but the next morning when he named his child for the first animal he saw when he looked from his tepee, his son instantly gained his eyesight. Everyone now believed him, and from that day to within recent years, the Indians have named their children after the first object they saw on looking from their tepees when a child was born.

The following day Wi-yuh disappeared to Guh-luh-lau-eeh.

Why the Turkey is Bald

(By Nan Saunooke, Cherokee, excerpted from *The Red Man*, Carlisle Indian School student newspaper, ca. 1925)

The Indians of our country have many legends connected with certain peculiar habits or customs prevalent among them. If one should chance to visit the home of an old Indian, he would perhaps notice a turkey wing hanging near the fire. This, the Indian uses to fan his fire into a flame and make it burn brightly, or perhaps in the sultry days of summer, to fan himself. If asked why he uses the turkey wing instead of the wing of any other bird, he would no doubt relate the following story:

Many years ago, the fire of the world was nearly extinguished; this happened just at the beginning of the winter season. The birds of the air were filled with anxiety, for their intuition told them they would need heat to keep them warm through the winter.

A bird council was held and it was decided that birds that could fly the highest should soar into the air and see if they could find a spark of fire anywhere. The efforts of the eagle, lark and raven were in vain. The honor was left to the little brown sparrow, who spied a spark of fire in the hollow of an old stump, in the heart of a deep forest.

The birds flocked around the stump and tried to decide who should pick the spark out. But all their efforts were in vain. To their dismay, they saw the spark growing smaller and fainter. The turkey then volunteered to try and keep the tiny coal alive by fanning it with his wings. Day after day, the turkey kept fanning; the heat became greater each day, until the feathers of the turkey's head were singed. If one notices carefully, he will see lumps on the head of a turkey that appear as blisters. It is believed that the turkey was so badly burned that all turkeys since, have had bald heads and wear the blisters as a memento of the bravery of the turkey. The faithful turkey lost his beautiful feathers, but he gave back fire to the world; so in his honor, and as a memorial of his faithfulness, the Indian uses the turkey wing to make his fire burn.

The Simple Happiness of a Navajo Girl

(Excerpt from Ann Clark, *Little Herder in Spring*, Bureau of Indian Affairs, Chilocco, Oklahoma, 1940)

My mother's hogan is dry
against the gray mists
of morning.

My mother's hogan is warm
against the gray cold
of morning.

I sit in the middle of its rounded walls,
walls that my father built
of juniper and good earth.

Walls that my father blessed
with song and corn pollen.
Here in the middle
of my mother's hogan
I sit
because I am happy.

HEADED FOR TOWN: This is how Navajo infants went to town and other places, riding on the backs of their mothers. The cradleboard has a sturdy leather strap fastened in back at about the baby's head, which the mother then wears over both shoulders and often grips with her hands at the front. The protective "roll-bar' on this cradleboard is decorated with designs made of wood, usually cotton-wood shaved to board thickness. The striped cloth draped over it becomes a screen dropped down in front of the baby's head when it's sleeping, or when flies and bugs get bothersome. The mother is wearing a fringed shawl over her long cloth dress.

Bibliography

Ann Clark, *Little Boy with Three Names*, Bureau of Indian Affairs, Chilocco, Oklahoma, 1940

Frank H. Cushing, *Zuni Folk Tales*, G. P. Putnam's Sons, New York, 1901

Frances Densmore, *Chippewa Customs*, Smithsonian Institution, Bureau of American Ethnology, Bulletin 86, Washington, DC 1929

Charles Alexander Eastman, *Indian Boyhood*, McClure, Phillips & Co., New York, 1902

Regina Flannery, *The Gros Ventres of Montana, Part 1, Social Life*, The Catholic University of America Press, Washington, DC 1953

Alice C. Fletcher and Francis La Flesche, *The Omaha Tribe*, vol. 2, Twenty-seventh Annual Report of the Bureau of Ethnology, Smithsonian Institution, Washington, DC, 1911

Robert H. Lowie, *Societies of the Crow*, American Museum of Natural History, New York, 1913

Robert H. Lowie, *Societies of the Hidatsa and Mandan Indians*, American Museum of Natural History, New York, 1913

Otis T. Mason, *Cradles of the American Aborigines*, Report of the National Museum, Smithsonian Institution, Washington, DC 1889

David G. Mandelbaum, "The Plains Cree," *Anthropological Papers of the American Museum of Natural History*, Volume xxxvii, Part II, New York City, 1940

James R. Murie, *Pawnee Indian Societies*, American Museum of Natural History, New York, 1914

Franc Johnson Newcomb, *Hosteen Klah*, University of Oklahoma Press, Norman, Oklahoma, 1964

Morris Edward Ogles, *An Apache Lifeway: The Economic, Social and Religious Institutions of Chiricahua Indians*, The University of Chicago Press, Chicago, IL 1941

Paul Radin, *The Winnebago Tribe*, Thirty-seventh Annual Report of the Bureau of American Ethnology, Smithsonian Institution, Washington, DC, 1923

Alanson Skinner, *Ponca Societies and Dances*, American Museum of Natural History, New York, 1915

Harry Holbert Turney-High, "The Flathead Indians of Montana," *Memoirs of the American Anthropological Association*, Number 48, Menasha, Wisconsin, 1937

Ruth Underhill, *Indians of the Pacific Northwest*, US Dept. of Interior, Bureau of Indian Affairs, Branch of Education, Washington, DC 1945

Gilbert L. Wilson, *Agriculture of the Hidatsa Indians: An Indian Interpretation*, Univ. of Minnesota Studies in the Social Sciences, No. 9, 1977

Gilbert L. Wilson, *The Horse and the Dog in Hidatsa Culture*, American Museum Press, New York, 1924

Clark Wissler, *Oglala Societies*, American Museum of Natural History, New York, 1916

Robert Young and William Morgan, *Coyote Tales*, Navajo Life Series, Bureau of Indian Affairs, Haskell Institute, Lawrence, Kansas, 1949

**Pow-Wow Dancer's
and Craftworker's
Handbook**
$19.95
978-1-57067-190-6

Traditional Dress
Knowledge & Methods of
Old-Time Clothing
$9.95
978-1-57067-147-0

Legends
Told by the Old People of
Many Tribes *(Rev. Ed.)*
$9.95
978-1-57067-116-6

**Indian Tribes of the
Northern Rockies**
$9.95
978-0-913990-74-2

Children of the Circle
Adolf & Star Hungry Wolf
$9.95
978-0-913990-89-6

Teachings of Nature
$8.95
978-0-913990-75-9

Purchase these Native American titles from your local bookstore
or you can buy them directly from:

Book Publishing Company • P.O. Box 99 • Summertown, TN 38483
1-800-695-2241
Please include $3.95 per book for shipping and handling.